THE CALLOWAY WAY

RESULTS & INTEGRITY

THE CALLOWAY WAY

RESULTS & INTEGRITY

WRITTEN BY

Charlie Feld
with David Hatch

FOREWORD BY

Indra K. Nooyi

FG PRESS | BOULDER, COLORADO

ART DIRECTOR | Kevin Barrett Kane

PEPSICO HQ PHOTOGRAPH | Joe Vericker

 FG PRESS, *Publishers*
ISBN 978-1-941018-09-5
$24.95 in the USA

DEDICATION

This book is dedicated to Jan and Wayne Calloway and the impact they had on me, my wife, Cindy, and thousands of our PepsiCo friends and family. We will forever be grateful.

CONTENTS

FOREWORD BY INDRA K. NOOYI

TIME AND DISTANCE CAN MAKE IT EASY TO ROMANTICIZE the contributions of business leaders and synthesize their management styles into a catchy phrase. Let me assure you, the "Calloway Way" is not such an example. When I joined PepsiCo twenty years ago, I was fortunate to have joined when Wayne Calloway was CEO. The "Calloway Way" was not only alive; it was tangible. It was shorthand for getting results with integrity—simply put, it meant effective leadership.

One of my favorite quotes from Wayne is "growth is oxygen." He knew that growth was the engine that made everything possible, and that adhering to the status quo was not an option. At times, that meant making big bets on strategic moves that would significantly change our business, but he also knew that standing still was the riskiest move of all.

Wayne's strategic vision helped propel PepsiCo forward, but he recognized that without the right talent to execute that vision, it would be all for naught. He understood at his very core that talent is the deciding factor that takes a company from good to great, and he lived it in his actions every day. He created a culture of positivity where people felt empowered to express their own unique perspectives—and in fact, he expected that everyone come prepared with a point of view. With this empowerment came a sense of ownership. PepsiCo was not just a company to us, it was our company. It's this environment that attracted the best and brightest to PepsiCo, and unsurprisingly, great business results followed.

As you read this book, I hope you will see that the "Calloway Way" was not just one man's successful approach to leadership at a specific point in time. It is a guide to the timeless and fundamental principles of leadership that have more application to us now than ever before. I treasured my time with Wayne and am so pleased to know that his legacy will be shared with everyone who reads this book.

Indra K. Nooyi
Chairman & CEO, PepsiCo
September 2014

INTRODUCTION

IF THIS BOOK WERE BEING WRITTEN 20 OR 30 YEARS AGO, few business observers would have argued with its basic premise, which is that Wayne Calloway was an exceptionally successful chief executive whose leadership model, strategic vision, and accomplishments, on a global scale, are worthy of attention and analysis. He guided PepsiCo, Inc. through a period of extraordinary transformation and achievement, enabling it to thrive in the most competitive of industries, all the while amassing a remarkable record of growth and performance. Throughout this period PepsiCo not only beat the market but almost always met the double-digit growth rate enshrined as the "PepsiCo Standard."

It was my privilege to work with Wayne, and to observe his management strategies first-hand, for more than 20 years. He was an exceptionally effective leader, and his leadership style and strategies have had a profound influence upon me throughout my career. In this, I am scarcely alone. For many of the executives who worked with Wayne at PepsiCo, or served with him elsewhere on corporate or nonprofit boards, he had a strong impact. He was the kind of business leader who made a difference.

I first met Wayne when I was a systems engineer at IBM. For 11 years, I was basically embedded, on a full-time basis, at Frito-Lay, Inc., serving as an IT consultant with involvement in every aspect of its business. After that, I went to work directly for PepsiCo, where I served as Frito-Lay's Chief Information Officer for another 11 years. In all, I was at PepsiCo from 1970 through 1992. During most of that time, I worked closely with Wayne. It was an exciting and unforgettable period.

During my tenure at PepsiCo, Wayne held a number of leadership roles of increasing importance. In the early days, he was the CFO of Frito-Lay, and he went on to serve as its CEO. Back then, Frito-Lay was relatively small, about $500 million in sales[1], but it was PepsiCo's most profitable division. What Wayne built at Frito-Lay was a world-class operation that consistently achieved exceptional results.

When he moved up to PepsiCo's headquarters in Purchase, New York, first as the corporation's CFO and then as its Chairman and CEO, he applied his leadership style and management strategies throughout the corporation, with an ever-expanding impact.

During this period, PepsiCo's revenues grew from $7.7 billion (1984)[2] to $30 billion (1995)[3] and, as is the case today, it was widely recognized and respected as one of the world's great corporations. To say that Wayne Calloway was highly regarded is an understatement. During his years at PepsiCo's helm, he was singled out as one of the world's most admired business leaders, with a strong following not only within PepsiCo's workforce, but throughout the global marketplace and the investment community as well.

In a 2014 conversation with Don Kendall—the legendary entrepreneur who was PepsiCo's cofounder, first Chairman and

CEO, and the man who hired and promoted Wayne through a number of key leadership positions—he talked about some of the reasons why Calloway was the right person to succeed him at the corporation's helm:

> Wayne did a very good job at Frito-Lay and then at PepsiCo. He had a great personality and intellect. He was a strong judge of people and a good salesman. He was optimistic and positive. A very nice guy—well-liked by everyone, from the employees to the customers. What more can I say except, these are all leadership qualities. He wasn't just a wonderful manager. He was a great friend, the kind of person that people respected, worked hard for, really loved.[4]

Wayne was a quiet but exceptional man who impacted others in many ways. Among his many achievements and accolades was winning President Ronald Reagan's prestigious Volunteer Action Award for his efforts—in support of the Dallas community where Frito-Lay was based—to find jobs for former Braniff Airlines employees who lost their jobs after the airline declared bankruptcy.

A graduate of Wake Forest University, Wayne remained deeply involved with the institution throughout his lifetime, serving as Chairman of its Board, and even finding the time to interview applicants whenever possible. In recognition of his extraordinary support and service, Wake Forest named its Calloway School of Business & Accountancy in Wayne's honor in 1995.

Jack Welch, the former CEO of GE, recalled in a 2014 interview for this book:

> I was a huge fan of Wayne's. My perspective on him comes from his role on GE's board, where he served as a director. He

was a man of few words. But when the bell rang on an important issue, he always spoke with clarity and conviction. He held the respect of everyone in the room. And within six months, he became one of the key members of our board.[5]

Management guru Tom Peters, who originally got to know Wayne when he worked on a McKinsey consulting engagement at Frito-Lay, put it simply: "If they hadn't invented the word 'decency,' they would have had to invent it for Wayne."[6]

He had a very clear and simple expectation for his leaders: Results and Integrity. When I say simple, I mean it's simple to understand but very difficult to do over a long period of time. I've watched many people fail because they were able to do both when times were good, but when there was trouble they would lean into one at the expense of the other. It is important to understand that when Calloway talked about integrity he didn't mean being honest—that was assumed. What he meant was intellectual integrity: Do you do what you say? Do you say what you mean? Can I trust you? Do you treat people with respect? Do your people trust you? He was very big on the idea that the "meeting should happen in the meeting." If you don't agree then say it in the room, not in the hallway.

He made the connection in his mind that the only way to drive sustainable results is if all those other traits are part of the character of both the individual and the organization. We will spend considerable time on this topic in Chapter 4, "Building a Great Team."

Wayne Calloway stepped down from PepsiCo's helm in 1996 because of health considerations, and he passed away two years later in 1998. Now, nearly 20 years later, his leadership strategies and accomplishments at PepsiCo have faded into the backdrop for many followers of the business world.

That is not surprising to those of us who worked with him closely and knew him well. He was a quiet man, and never the type of executive who tried to capture attention or claim credit. He devoted his time and energies to his professional and personal commitments rather than to building and spreading his reputation. He chose not to be a celebrity, a media superstar, or a management guru. He derived his satisfaction from watching the hundreds of PepsiCo leaders blossom.

Since Wayne was scarcely the kind of corporate executive who would ever sit down and write a book about himself, one might ask why have I taken it upon myself to carry out this project, and why now? I thought I had written my first and last book when I published *Blind Spot: A Leader's Guide to IT-Enabled Business Transformation* in 2010.[7]

That said, I have embarked on this project with two motivations in mind. First, businesses are currently undergoing a period of massive, technology-driven change and transformation—and we as individuals, corporations, and countries are all struggling to cope with complex and difficult challenges. We are sorely in need of a renaissance in leadership, and Wayne Calloway's leadership model and accomplishments offer important lessons for us all.

Second, I seek to chronicle a strong and successful leader, who navigated a great corporation through an exciting period of growth and accomplishment, all while influencing and inspiring a large group of executives, including myself, to prosper in PepsiCo's nonstop talent machine.

I've collaborated on this project with David Hatch, with whom I've worked over the past 30 years. He worked closely with me as my Management Development partner at Frito-Lay. Eventually, he became the Vice President of Management Development for PepsiCo. In this role, he traveled extensively with Wayne while he was Chairman and CEO. David provided tremendous enthusiasm and many insights for this project.

FraserWalbert Media LLC, a strategic communications and multimedia marketing firm, provided valuable editorial services throughout this project. I am grateful for their support.

Before concluding this introduction, I must offer my appreciation to Wayne's cherished wife, Jan Calloway, who was his valued partner through many years in Frito-Lay's and PepsiCo's top management ranks. Without Jan's involvement and support, this book would have never been possible. She shared her memories, loaned copies of Wayne's speeches and taped interviews, and helped connect us with other executives who offered their own perspective on the Wayne Calloway leadership model. Thanks Jan for helping keep his memory alive for all of us.

It is a great challenge, as well as a responsibility, to attempt to translate the leadership strategies and accomplishments of an admired colleague and friend—especially one who is no longer with us—into the pages of a book. I do so, with the deepest of respect for Wayne and our heritage organization, PepsiCo.

Charlie Feld
Founder, The Feld Group Institute
Dallas, September 2014

THE CALLOWAY WAY

RESULTS & INTEGRITY

CHAPTER ONE
A RENAISSANCE IN LEADERSHIP

FEW PEOPLE WOULD ARGUE that these are challenging times, ripe with opportunities and promise. Yet risks abound. Socioeconomic problems persist. Even as our knowledge continues to increase exponentially, we find ourselves all too often unable to make sense of the ever more complex world in which we live and work. Every generation probably felt this way to a degree. But something very different is going on now. The speed and breadth of change is stunning and old solutions are not working.

Many business and political leaders are stuck looking in the rear-view mirror. They don't have a broad enough context to help us move forward into a complex future that is being shaped, and in many ways redefined, by innovative new technologies. Creating an exciting and positive future will require a real Renaissance in Leadership.

Whether for corporations that are struggling to respond to those disruptive technologies and unparalleled levels of competition, or for countries that must figure out how to leverage new solutions and reinvent education, healthcare, energy, food supplies and systems, security, privacy, and more, the need for effective leadership with a deep understanding of *why* to change and how to set new agendas has never been more pressing.

NEW AGENDAS – WHY LEADERSHIP MATTERS

Let's start with the basic context that in previous eras, just as today, technological advances drove change and transformation.

The invention of the printing press, the internal combustion engine, and the telegraph all changed the way we live, learn, work, travel, and communicate, as surely as the personal computer, the Internet, and the smartphone have done in recent years. Yet there are two fundamental differences between this current stage of technology-driven transformation and anything mankind previously has experienced.

The first relates to the breathtaking pace at which new technologies are being developed and adopted. Long ago, this might have spanned centuries, and then generations. Although it's easy to forget this, even the automobile, telephone, and electricity took decades to achieve widespread adoption and a truly transformational impact.

When transformations happen over a long period of time, individuals, institutions, and economic and political systems can adjust. As our industrial revolution progressed over the last 200 years, "about 90% of Americans worked in agriculture in 1800; by 1900 it was 41%, and by 2000 it was just 2%. As workers left farms over the course of two centuries, there were more than enough new jobs created in other sectors, and whole new industries sprang up to employ them."[1]

Now, the adoption rate for new technologies is measured in years or even months, which means that very big changes are taking place within increasingly compressed periods of time. The technology curve (Moore's Law) may have made the smartphone predictable from the perspective of technological advances. However, the adoption curve that smartphones experienced—mass distribution in less than five years—changed everything from commerce to social and political landscapes, which was unparalleled.

Meanwhile, just as the pace of technology-driven change has gotten so much faster, the second major difference between now and the past relates to the geographic breadth—that is, the magnitude of global impact—that can be achieved by new technologies very quickly, thanks to their price and availability. As we saw with the smartphone, every part of the globe can be impacted rapidly, as new innovations get widely adopted almost at the same time worldwide.

The current pattern is in stark contrast with the historical experience of technology-driven transformation, which typically emanated from one location only to radiate slowly to other regions across the globe, often over the course of many decades. It took years, for example, after the automobile was invented, for car ownership to spread beyond a relatively tiny number of individuals and transform our rhythm of life.

Yet today, unlike in the past, massive technology-driven changes can take place in one part of the globe within an extremely short window of time and quickly spread throughout every geographic region and to all levels of society. The implications of all this can literally seem inconceivable—until they happen. Who would have imagined that the rapid, worldwide adoption of the smartphone, Facebook, Twitter, instant messaging, and YouTube would create tumultuous societal changes across the globe in a matter of months?

In this new world of ours, it can seem as though the very elements of time and space are shifting around us. After all, when it comes to technology-driven change, time keeps shrinking while the space (or geographic) dimension has expanded. This is exciting but can also be disorienting, confusing, frightening, and even overwhelming.

Now, let's think about all this in a larger context. During the same period when the adoption curve for new technology was ramping up exponentially (with the iPhone and iPad introduced in 2007 and 2010, respectively),[2] the great global recession happened. So we had two huge changes taking place at the same time, and the result was extraordinary confusion about what was happening and why.

Business, political, and social leaders alike have tended to confuse the downturn with a more fundamental structural shift. Large numbers of jobs inevitably would have gone away as technology replaced people and as communications and information technology became more massively available.

> Today, over 2.5 billion people have digital cameras and the vast majority of photos are digital. The effects are astonishing...A team of just fifteen people at Instagram created a simple app that over 130 million customers use to share some sixteen billion photos...Contrast these figures with pre-digital behemoth Kodak...Kodak employed 145,300 people... while indirectly employing thousands more via the extensive supply chain and retail distribution channels required by companies in the first machine age...We've created a cornucopia of images, sharing nearly four hundred billion "Kodak

moments" each year with a few clicks of a mouse or taps on a screen. But companies like Instagram and Facebook employ a tiny fraction of the people that were needed at Kodak.[3]

So, even if the "catalytic" downturn of 2008–09 had not happened, we would have experienced major disruptions, similar to the kind of shifts that occurred during earlier periods of technology-driven change. Granted, the change would have been a little more gradual, but it would have happened all the same.

Yet it is still conventional wisdom that the global downturn caused massive unemployment and profound disruptions to our institutions. This assumption, that it is a "disruption" vs. a structural shift, is dangerous and can lead to a mindset that says we need to do more of what worked during the last downturn. This lens dictates that we need to utilize public policies that stimulate the economy and lower interest rates, so as to "fix the system" in the way that we might have done in the past. It is more than reasonable, however, to assume that the "new reality" is very different from what has been in the past, and that old fixes may actually be accelerating inevitable corporate and municipal bankruptcies as well as market and geopolitical turmoil.

Although it's certainly the case that the global economic downturn exacerbated problems such as unemployment and dislocation, it's also true that even without that downturn, the pace and magnitude of technology-driven change would have produced major structural changes worldwide. After all, once transformative new technologies have gained widespread adoption, there's no turning back. That's why public policy interventions, while critical to stabilize the "system," can prove ineffective at fixing the structural issues. We might have a good grasp of the "facts," but leaders at all levels may be missing the "system" causes.

What will the future be like, even five years from now? Moore's Law dictates that the pace of all this technology-driven change will only continue to accelerate. As complexities mount and our challenges continue to increase, individuals, organizations, and countries themselves will need the resiliency and agility to adjust. We will also need new agendas to help us to capitalize upon the win-win opportunities that technology can provide to empower consumers, create healthier and better educated populations, and accomplish much more.

The potential upside is vast and, as is clear, there is no turning backwards. Yet, at a time when the entire world seems to be evolving at hyper-speed, individuals, enterprises, and governments alike often lack the perspective to understand what's happening and why, to visualize and pursue meaningful longer-term goals, and to work together towards solving the many problems that still confront us.

I would submit that yes, we do have economic, political, and social crises on a global scale, and yes, there *will* be winners and losers. Yet despite the magnitude of any particular problem, I contend that the biggest crisis in the world today is a crisis of leadership at many levels. You can't fix what you don't understand. You can't inspire what you can't imagine, and you can't motivate change if you can't lead. We, for sure, have financial, employment, education, healthcare, security, and energy deficits. But I would argue that our most critical deficit is a clear view of the current reality, a compelling and exciting view of what is possible in the future, and the will and grit to get from here to there.

John Micklethwait and Adrian Wooldridge put it well in their book, *The Fourth Revolution: The Global Race to Reinvent the State,* when they wrote:

> Now these questions are discussed only in piecemeal form. Modern politicians are like architects arguing about the condition of individual rooms in a crumbling house, rushing to fix a window here or slap on a new coat of paint there, without even considering the design of the whole building. We need to look at the design of the whole structure.[4]

That's what leadership can provide to us, and that is why leadership matters so much at every level.

* * *

We've created a world of empowered consumer-citizens. They may be comparison shoppers who are seeking to spend as little money as possible or consumers of blogs, or gamers, or online students whose classroom interactions take place through smartphones or tablets. They have many options in this new world to learn, to play, to create, to destroy, to cure or to harm. The bottom line is, individuals are now in charge. As they've gained control, institutions have lost it. Leaders who recognize this are taking steps to help their organizations adjust to this new reality. But leaders who stick their heads in the sand and assume that old institutional, educational or industrial frameworks will once again suffice, as soon as the economic recovery "really picks up steam," will soon find that they, and their organizations, are obsolete.

What we've got now is an overall environment in which change is taking place at a dizzying pace. Everything is in motion all the time. In addition to the "Internet of People," there is an explosion of the "Internet of Things," which includes sensors, chips, cameras,

GPS devices, and so forth, which are being embedded in products that can be used for good or possibly evil purposes.

Within this environment, we've got all these empowered consumer-citizens, whose behavior is being driven by the technologies that they adopt and the choices that they're making about consumption. At the end of the day, these technologically-empowered men and women win, since they get what they want, when they want it, and usually at lower prices. But the flip side, whether for corporations, universities, and all kinds of other institutions, is that these organizations will need to figure out how to reinvent their strategic models in an environment in which everything will continue to change, and cycle time to react will continue to compress.

The good news is, technology holds the potential to empower enterprises to better understand their constituents, significantly improve customer service, more effectively manage their supply chains, and so forth. But the race will be on to innovate more rapidly, drive down costs, and compete more effectively for constituents who have exponentially greater choices.

Within this new and rapidly shifting environment, policy makers and lobbyists might try to introduce more barriers, but the empowered consumer is usually going to choose to spend $10 for a T-shirt rather than $50. New technologies make it easier all the time for consumers to buy what they want, where they want, and when they want. In a global marketplace like this one, retailers will keep shifting the burden of cost-savings down the line to their suppliers, while seeking ways to distinguish themselves. In the end, consumers will get better prices, products, and services—which is a terrific result.

Business has always been about competition and there have

always been winners and losers. But a realistic look at today's situation reveals that some significant problems are inevitable. The pace of business has changed. It's much faster and more brutal, and it can be extremely punishing, especially to any publicly traded corporation that doesn't achieve its targeted results in the short term.

Within this context, what's critical is a change-oriented mindset. Institutions and individuals alike will need to embrace change and to cultivate agility. We no longer have the luxury of getting used to conditions that shift over decades or even generations. Those that resist this reality will struggle because, as they say, if you don't like change, you're going to hate extinction.

Weak companies will continue to fall off the map. Strong companies will continue to embrace and leverage this technology era. In either case, there will be more people looking for fewer jobs of the sort that flourished in the Industrial Era. The jobs in this century will require different skills. This will have increasingly severe repercussions for businesses and individuals that prove unable or unwilling to acquire these new skills.

Unfortunately, even as individuals and institutions are struggling to find the right footing within this rapidly shifting arena, our leaders are often responding to quarterly stock market pressures, or the next election, or results of the latest polls. Because they don't understand the systemic changes, the overall nature of technology-driven transformation, and the potential for unintended consequences, they keep reaching for strategies that might have once worked but are now utterly inappropriate. That can be worse than simply ineffective, since these misguided attempts may end up exacerbating difficult conditions and creating a whole new set of pressures as problems mount.

For example, by keeping interest rates so low, the central banks have provided institutions with capital to invest in new technologies and modernize plants, facilities, and equipment; but regulations that increase costs, reduce flexibility, or raise minimum wages all encourage spending on modernizing machines, not people. Again, this has huge ramifications for all of us, since machines may sell hamburgers, and they may even cook hamburgers all by themselves one day, but they will never walk into a restaurant to buy and eat them.

Many companies are struggling right now, whether because they didn't see change coming, or they saw it coming but didn't know how to deal with it, or they saw change coming and had a plan, but didn't move quickly enough to achieve meaningful results. It can be tempting to throw up one's hands in despair during a period like this one—to focus on the widespread confusion and crisis in leadership—rather than focus on the potential for a leadership renaissance and the great value that leaders with clarity and vision could bring to the table.

But for someone like me, who spent 22 years working in the PepsiCo system with Wayne Calloway, that kind of cynicism or "victim's mentality" is simply inconceivable. What he expected was a focus on reality, rather than a sense that life was either worse or better than it was. If you were on the PepsiCo team, you needed to understand today's facts, look ahead to assess the challenges and the opportunities, come up with solutions, and then make them happen. That's what it meant to be a leader, and it was Wayne's goal to empower people throughout the organization to adopt that kind of mindset. If you either didn't have a sense of reality or you were realistic but simply despairing, then you couldn't be successful at PepsiCo.

Fast-forwarding to today, the specific facts and challenges may be different, but the basic leadership principles are still the same. We need to trade in those rear-view mirrors for telescopes that enable us to, first, zoom in to get a realistic sense of our current situation: an understanding of which ways an organization's heritage may be an asset or liability in this new world. Then, we need to zoom out to figure out what needs to change and why, and as importantly, what needs to stay the same. That agenda-setting capability was a major success factor for any PepsiCo leader.

Because leaders like Wayne knew how to use both ends of the telescope, their teams knew how to focus on what they needed to achieve in the short-run—that's a given—but they were always focused as well on achieving those results that would matter most over time.

These are tough times, and individuals, companies, and governments will all need to find ways to reinvent themselves to keep up with the rapid pace of change and intense levels of competition. I believe that we can accomplish this, but we need the kind of leaders who can help us face and respond to new realities.

Wayne never used a smartphone. He passed away nearly ten years before these devices entered the market and rapidly transformed the ways that we live and work. Yet I am absolutely confident that he would have risen to today's challenges (while inspiring those who worked with him to do the same), because he would have had the clarity and vision to recognize and respond to the competitive dynamics created by new technologies and by a marketplace dominated by empowered consumers.

* * *

At this point, I hope we can agree with the quote commonly attributed to Albert Einstein that it is "insanity" to keep doing the same thing over and over again but expect different results. We can be victims of this accelerated change or we can reimagine new possibilities and solutions. Make no mistake. Of all the things that matter now, leadership matters the most. We need leaders who are capable of being realistic in their understanding of the current state and are also able to understand a future that is both positive and possible. These leaders will possess the management expertise and experience necessary for "Setting the Agenda" (Ch. 2) that is, to establish the directional coordinates that will guide the journey from where we are to where we need to be.

They will also recognize the essential importance of "Building a Great Team" (Ch. 4) and inspiring a culture of commitment and accountability. And, finally, as all effective leaders must do, they will be oriented toward showing results and progress over time, that is, "Delivering with Consistency" (Ch. 3). This was the Calloway magic formula: three core leadership expectations that were embedded within our organizational culture and rooted in values and integrity.

The book focuses on these key leadership components within PepsiCo, our heritage corporation and truly, one of the world's great business organizations. It was and is a very special place that developed leaders who, over many years, have had a huge impact throughout the global business community.

In addition, it will examine, in greater detail, the timeless leadership "system" that made Wayne Calloway such a special and impactful leader of leaders. He made it his life's work for more than 25 years, including his terms as the head of Frito-Lay and then as the CEO of PepsiCo, to inspire people to set an agenda, build a great team, and deliver with consistency.

As so many of us struggle with the limitations of today's leadership—whether in corporations, other institutions, or political systems—and seek a renaissance in leadership, the timeless principles embodied by Wayne Calloway and the great company he led hold much value today.

NOTES

1. Andrew McAfee and Erik Brynjolfsson, *Race Against The Machine* (Lexington, Mass: Digital Frontier Press, 2011), p. 49.

2. "Apple Reinvents the Phone with iPhone," Apple, https://www.apple.com/pr/library/2007/01/09Apple-Reinvents-the-Phone-with-iPhone.html and "Apple Launches iPad," Apple, https://www.apple.com/pr/library/2010/01/27Apple-Launches-iPad.html.

3. Erik Brynjolfsson and Andrew McAfee, *The Second Machine Age: Work, Progress, and Prosperity in a Time of Brilliant Technologies* (New York: W.W. Norton & Company, 2014), p.126-127.

4. John Micklethwait and Adrian Wooldridge, *The Fourth Revolution: The Global Race to Reinvent the State* (New York:The Penguin Press, 2014), p. 21.

CHAPTER TWO
SETTING THE AGENDA

IN CHAPTER 1, I FOCUSED ON THE "WHY." I examined our current challenges and made a case for why I believe a leadership renaissance is required at all levels.

The remainder of the book will focus on the "how," by examining in greater detail a timeless, well-tested leadership model that is based upon three key elements: Setting the Agenda, Delivering with Consistency, and Building a Great Team. This model can be applied to both public and private enterprises, and it has relevance for leaders throughout an organization and in a broad range of fields, from C-suite executives to field officers to high-ranking government officials.

It works.

My belief in the value of this leadership model is steeped in my long-time experiences at PepsiCo, which was one of the great corporate leadership development academies. The nearly two decades that I spent there were foundational years for me. Although I have spent in total nearly five decades working in business, I still consider that period to have been an extraordinarily influential, exciting, and intellectually rewarding time.

At PepsiCo, I was surrounded by leaders at every level. The institutional model bred and encouraged that type of leadership mentality, rooted in the three-part strategic model that I outlined above. It produced decades of exceptional performance, year in and year out.

This PepsiCo model was carefully and purposefully built over the course of these decades by many terrific and successful people. But the driver of all this was Wayne Calloway, who truly was a leader of leaders. As mentioned, I met him in 1970, when I was in my mid-20s and serving as an IBM Systems Engineer assigned to Frito-Lay. He was in his mid-30s and already the CFO at the division, PepsiCo's most profitable one. From the day I met him until the day he retired as Chairman and CEO of PepsiCo, Wayne never changed in two crucial characteristics: his competitive fire and his kind, caring approach to people at every level of the organization.

Donald R. Keough, who served as President of Coca-Cola during the same era in which Wayne led PepsiCo, once described him as "a fierce competitor and really a true and noble gentleman," adding, "It's a rare combination."[1] Steve Reinemund, who worked with Wayne for many years, including as the CEO of Pizza Hut, described him this way:

> Wayne was a ferocious competitor, but in a disarming way. He was an emotional, inspiring, and truly motivational leader. If I were to put a title on his approach, I would call it, 'win with integrity.' He was always clear on what was most important.[2]

Throughout Wayne Calloway's career, he remained completely focused on the core themes that this book describes. In fact, the reason why I consider him to be such an important leadership archetype is that, during his long career at PepsiCo, which he joined in 1967, he managed to set and achieve very big agendas not once but continuously. He did this first at the divisional level, at Frito-Lay, where he served in leadership roles from 1970 to 1983, and then for the corporation as a whole during the years between 1983 and 1996. Most significantly, he accomplished this with an extraordinary and unusual degree of consistency over the course of two and a half decades in top leadership roles.

Throughout these pages, we will examine the way that he accomplished these exceptional results by encouraging the success of others throughout the organization. As CEO, he was the driving force behind PepsiCo's honored and often-imitated "Leadership Academy," which truly was a nonstop talent machine. In his belief that leadership matters, he was part of a long and noble tradition at PepsiCo. Successful entrepreneurs and cofounders, Herman Lay and Don Kendall (who served as the corporation's first CEO), nurtured this approach, and Andrall (Andy) Pearson (the former McKinsey & Company partner who served as PepsiCo's first President) was the architect. However, Wayne institutionalized this approach and made it an integral part of PepsiCo's management strategy and everyday work life. And he maintained this priority, decade after decade.

One of Wayne's extraordinary skills as a leader was his ability to encourage people at all levels of the organization to think and act like leaders themselves, from the corporate and divisional C-suites all the way through to the restaurant managers and route salesmen who had the closest perspective on consumer preferences. Elsewhere in this book, we will examine the ways that Wayne sought to reinforce this priority through an employee stock ownership program that was truly innovative for its time. His belief was that everyone should approach his or her job like an owner.

But, for now, I'll conclude by stating simply: As the Calloway leadership model (and the leadership mindset) were replicated at all levels throughout the PepsiCo community, the value of this approach was demonstrated in countless ways, helping PepsiCo to achieve a truly extraordinary record of success.

SETTING THE AGENDA

Leaders at all levels set an agenda, whether they realize this or not. In fact, the very act of not setting an agenda effectively creates an agenda for an organization. An agenda may be small, tactically focused on surviving the day or the week, or it can be large and strategically focused on winning the future. A successful leader can cover both kinds of objectives, by having an "and/and" not an "either/or" perspective.

More specifically, it really matters when good leaders are able to conceive and articulate a strong and positive vision of the future. This enables people to strive towards a goal that is inspiring and clear, and it motivates them to put their mind, spirit, and body into the effort. That said, being able to survive in the short term is also critical. Without short- and medium-term results you and your organization cannot survive. That's why an "and/and" leadership approach is essential.

Weak leaders tend to adopt an "either/or" orientation. They spend all their time on one end of a telescope or the other. They're either focused on the near-term lens: that is, the effort to struggle forward every day, month or year, without any particular longer-term direction in mind. Or else, their telescope is focused on the long-term perspective: that is, they "dream" big visions about the future, with no practical pathway to get from here to there.

Perhaps they lack the "grit" to do what's necessary to achieve the longer-term targets. Or, they might overlook the near-term perspective entirely, and fail to focus on current priorities that are also absolutely essential.

Whether I refer to this as the "and/and" leadership mindset or describe it as utilizing both lenses of the telescope, this dual strategic management perspective is extremely important. After all, any type of change is a journey from where you are to where you aspire to be. Presumably, that future state is an attractive one, which will make the journey worth the effort. But you need to be able to deliver day in and day out if you are to survive and prosper.

ARTICULATING THE FUTURE

One reason Wayne Calloway was as effective as he was in inspiring people throughout PepsiCo was his whole-hearted, passionate commitment to a simple and eloquent articulation of who we were and what we aspired to be: a growth company.

For him, "Setting the Agenda" started with one large, overarching priority: growth. PepsiCo's Chairman and CEO, Indra Nooyi, told us that her favorite quote of Wayne's was, "Growth is oxygen."[3] Indeed, throughout his leadership years, first at Frito-Lay and then at PepsiCo, Wayne established huge growth targets, which included double-digit annual increases and high margins, with limited capital spending and a relentless focus on achieving these results, with consistency, year after year.

To Wayne Calloway, it seemed clear that a growth-oriented agenda was at the heart of PepsiCo's very corporate being. During a speech before an audience of business students at Sacred Heart University in June 1994, he explained:

PepsiCo by its very nature is a growth company. A deep and abiding commitment to growth has been fundamental to PepsiCo since our earliest days. You see, PepsiCo was formed by the merger of Pepsi and Frito-Lay. That was back in 1965... both companies already were successful and had bright futures all their own. But they wanted a lot more. They wanted to be a fast-growing, vibrant, important player. So they merged, and then hired people who shared that drive, who in turn hired others who saw growth as all-important. So the bias for growth has been with us from the start.

In a 1995 speech before the Food Marketing Institute, he emphasized:

Without growth, we eventually perish. It may be five years. It may be 50. But eventually, a non-growing business withers and dies. Nobody with real ambition goes to work there. The good ideas and good people go elsewhere. You're always back on your heels defending and blocking. In the long run, you can't live that way.

During more than 25 years in leadership roles at PepsiCo, Wayne Calloway set and pursued an agenda that demonstrated what was possible when growth was at the heart of the corporate mission. It fuelled greatness. In that same speech to the Food Marketing Institute, he commented:

For 40 years, PepsiCo averaged 16% a year. Imagine 40 years. That's pretty good, but what's far more important, over that time, our return to shareholders was almost identical....

Lots of people really do believe that you can have either

sales growth or profitability, but not both. But if you look at the Fortune list, you see something different. Vigorous, long-term sales growth is essential to vigorous long-term profitability. You can't have one without the other. The reason, in my opinion is the cultural implication of growth. It feeds on itself, attracting the best people, and they, in turn, drive greater success.

Joe McCann, who worked with Wayne for many years, in roles that included serving as PepsiCo's Senior Vice President of Public Affairs, commented:

> Wayne had great insight into both business and people. At PepsiCo, he focused on businesses that were capable of exceptional growth: 'If you pinch them, they'll jump.' To produce exceptional results, he had to find people that could make that happen. He looked for executives to lead the business, not just manage it.[4]

Working at PepsiCo during this era was certainly challenging and demanding, but it was exciting and, quite honestly, it was a lot of fun. Here's how Wayne himself described the process in a July speech before Sacred Heart University's business students:

> We set very ambitious goals for our managers, goals that drive us to be much more aggressive in the marketplace than a company content with modest or slow growth—to constantly come up with bigger, more creative ideas that make consumers sit up and take notice. And each year, as our challenge grows, we have to respond in bigger and better ways...To achieve really big growth requires an extraordinarily aggressive approach,

stretch goals, thinking in much grander terms than ordinary companies, working relentlessly to improve upon a performance that would leave other businesses feeling pretty content.

Joe McCann was reminded of a story told to him by a former colleague—it's one that many of us who worked closely with Wayne could relate to:

> You would go in to see Wayne with your plan for the year and say, "Here's the plan. I think we could do this, and that, and we could grow profits by 8%." And Wayne would say, "Well, that's nice." And then he'd sit there and not say anything. And you would sit there and not say anything, but you'd be thinking. So after a while, you'd say, "Well, OK, Wayne, maybe I could do this or that during the year and we could make 9%." Then he'd say, "Oh, that's interesting."
>
> And then he'd sit there and you both would be quiet, but you'd be thinking about what you could try. And finally, you'd say, "OK Wayne. I've got a plan and I'll do 12%." And that would be Wayne. He would drag you up there to where he wanted you and your team to be in terms of growth. But he wouldn't do that by telling you what the plan should be. He would scarcely say anything at all. But he would let you know what he thought was right for your team and the corporation itself. And it was truly phenomenal what he could get you to achieve.[5]

Bill Bensyl, who served as Senior Vice President of Human Resources during this period commented:

> You always felt when there was an action to be taken that you

owned the outcome. He listened, didn't interrupt, he would ask insightful questions, and get everyone's point of view. You never had to be concerned if you had his full support. Once decided, he rode to the finish line with you.[6]

Setting an agenda with short- and long-term goals is a prerequisite for success. Within PepsiCo, every leader throughout the organization knew what was expected of his or her team and understood the way that this fit into the overall institutional agenda. The power of the agenda rested in its absolute clarity.

Meanwhile, Wayne Calloway made sure that PepsiCo's key external constituents also appreciated the organization's clarity of purpose. Here's an excerpt from a speech that he delivered at the September 1994 Prudential Conference in Boston, detailing core elements of the PepsiCo growth strategy:

Our primary goal is long term and consistent profit growth of 15%... To achieve that broad single objective, we have the following specific goals: First, we expect the primary driver of our growth to be real volume. We don't rely on pricing to grow the bottom line, nor do we believe that you can save your way to prosperity.

Second, we expect all three businesses to grow. One should not support the other, at least not over the long term. Third, we expect all our investments to achieve cash returns of 14% or more. Our cost of capital is 11%. If we earn more than the cost of capital, we're adding to shareholder value. The 14% gives us a margin for error. Fourth, we expect each line of business to generate free cash. This means they should be able to cover their own needs for capital spending and still throw off cash for acquisitions, even when growing aggressively. Fifth, we expect to maintain an interest coverage ratio of more than four times. We use debt aggressively, but by focusing on cash flow, this is achievable.

THE JOURNEY TO THE FUTURE

With growth as the center of the Calloway Leadership Agenda, major initiatives such as "Double in Place," "Zero Defects," and "The Perfect Order" were rallying points that helped the institution stay aligned and achieving target objectives.

Speaking from the perspective of someone who worked inside PepsiCo for over 20 years, I can testify first-hand that these and other growth-oriented initiatives were difficult, they were demanding, and it was absolutely inspiring to be part of making them happen. Leaders and teams at all levels throughout the organization were striving for excellence and we were absolutely focused on achieving the agenda that our CEO established, over both the short- and the long-term.

Strong leaders embrace the vision and understand that the journey will require change. No matter how successful an organization may be today, it must be prepared for that change. And the way that this happens is through constant open dialogue and adaptation. During a speech that Wayne Calloway gave at the H.W. Lay Leadership Forum in Dallas in September 1995, he said:

How will the consumer change over the next few years, and what should we do about it? These are questions we have to ask and respond to every single day. But the reality is, no matter what we predict today, it's likely to be at least partially wrong. Consumers change. Furthermore, they don't always know what they want...My point is, no matter how well you predict, you're dealing with a moving target.

Every journey requires knowledge of two things, the destination and the starting point. Great leaders understand the current state, which is where their organizations are right now. Calloway was always focused on understanding whatever the reality was that PepsiCo and its different divisions and managers were confronting. That was an absolute starting point for him, and he engrained this focus in leaders at all levels throughout the organization.

During that same speech at the H.W. Lay Leadership Forum, he provided an illuminating window into the multifaceted process that helped him, and leaders throughout the PepsiCo organization, to develop a realistic understanding of the corporation's current state:

> The single greatest danger for a big successful company is "inside focus." The single greatest opportunity: "outside focus." There is no great company without "outside focus."...It's thinking about consumers, rather than yourself. It's thinking about consumer needs rather than organizational needs. It's thinking about our customers rather than our careers. It's really adapting the business and ourselves to the reality of the marketplace rather than doing the opposite, forcing ourselves on an unwilling world....The best example is an old one, the American auto industry of the '60s and '70s. They were so full of themselves, so obsessed by their own power, they missed a little thing called the Japanese [auto industry].

As that auto industry example makes clear, it can be quite a challenge for a corporation or any other institution to develop a realistic sense of its current state. It can be all too simple to get confused by irrelevant details, defensive emotions, and fear. But I believe that great leaders are adept at absorbing the facts and assessing reality in an insightful, unemotional, and balanced way, without placing blame or credit. Difficult as this might be to believe, this is an art.

It takes a lot of skill and experience to develop this art, but one essential skill is the ability to listen to others. In that, Wayne was a master. As anyone who ever knew him will be quick to describe, he was not much of a talker. But in his interactions with others, he embodied a maxim that he often used: "God gave you two ears and one mouth, and they should be used accordingly."

Roger King, Wayne's Head of Human Resources, described this as "intense listening." PepsiCo's Chairman and CEO, Indra Nooyi, who worked with him early in her career at the corporation, described Wayne's strengths in this regard:

> He managed meetings very effectively. He would allow everyone to engage in a discussion. He would not cut people off. He would skillfully ask the right questions to move a discussion along and to shape the outcome. He was a very good problem solver, in large part because of this ability to listen and to gather all of the facts from different points of view before coming to an understanding and reaching a decision.[7]

Tom Peters observed a similar strength:

> There may be no more significant strategic competence than the ability to listen to your people, to your customers. You have to learn how to keep quiet and let the other guy talk, and I really believe that. Wayne was a master at that.[8]

As we think about this notion of the "current state" and the challenges that are involved with developing an accurate understanding of it, let me step back for a moment and observe something about human nature. Most people approach life in one of two ways. The first is the pessimist who thinks, "What a mess I inherited. How could anyone (or any group) be so stupid? This is impossible to fix." The second is the optimist who thinks, "It's not so bad. This problem is nobody's fault. We can fix anything."

Both approaches are problematic and, frankly, counter-productive. Effective leadership adopts another course, which represents a distinctly different approach. Successful leaders like Calloway are grounded in reality, and they are adept at communicating the necessary messages about that reality, right down the emotional center line.

In a nutshell, they know how to grasp and convey, "It is what it is." That simple message is often ripe with meaning: "This is where we are for a whole host of root-cause reasons. Just as a balance sheet gives us a snapshot sense of our assets and liabilities, these are the facts, positive and negative, associated with our current situation. This is our starting point. We own it together."

There's so much meaning bound up in an attitude like that one. But perhaps nothing is more important than the message about jointly owning the starting point. Successful leaders appreciate that, when they set an agenda, its prospects for success depend heavily upon men and women throughout the organization or institution sharing an understanding and ownership of the current reality.

This reality, shared and articulated in a clear, concise framework that the organization is able to absorb, accept, and embrace, will serve as the anchor point of any agenda going forward. I would argue that accomplishing this is absolutely essential for any leader in any field of endeavor. Although it should be the easiest part of setting the agenda, it is remarkable how relatively few leaders that I have observed or interacted with in my post-PepsiCo career are able to do this properly.

There are a number of reasons why the shared understanding of the current situation is so elusive to many leaders. The most typical is that they don't want to hear it. That manifests itself in a few cultural issues. Frequently, these leaders simply refuse to make themselves available to hear a broad range of opinions. They surround themselves with people that tell them what they think they want to hear rather than what they need to know. Or they have a tendency to "shoot the messenger." This was the opposite in Calloway's PepsiCo.

The ability to listen attentively, grasp the facts, not place blame, and own the problem all came together for me after Wayne hired me to be the CIO at Frito-Lay in 1981. During the 1970s, Frito-Lay had four different CIOs that all left for different reasons. I was the fifth and was not interested in a "two-year career." Since I had been the IBM onsite representative at Frito-Lay during that decade I was very familiar with the problems that each of them struggled with. However, I wanted an independent third party to help me create a current state "balance sheet" for IT. Wayne agreed and I hired an IT specialty firm started by Dick Nolan and Dave Norton (Nolan/Norton), two Harvard professors. They brought in a great team led by Bruce Rogow and Bill Kelvie. Their process was to assess our assets and liabilities in a fact-based framework they had developed and then to place us on a maturity curve. At the end of about a 90-day engagement they presented their assessment to Wayne; Mike Jordan, Senior VP of Operations; Bill

Korn, Senior VP of Sales and Marketing; and me. It was a full-day off-site session with a dinner and a brief wrap-up the next morning. There were no surprises for me, but they had framed up the issues around the typical elements: Technology, Cost, Quality, Speed, Organization issues and Governance in a way that was digestible to a non-IT executive. Mike, Bill and the Nolan/Norton team were very active and engaged during Day 1, arguing, debating root causes, possible solutions, etc. The fact that Wayne was virtually silent during the first day didn't alarm anyone on the Frito-Lay team, but on the way to dinner Dick Nolan asked me if he was bored or disappointed or even paying attention. I assured him that he was very engaged and attentively listening—that was just Calloway.

The next morning he got to a flipchart and in a very concise and unassuming way said he "thinks" this is what he heard: We have technology issues, cost, quality, high turnover, bad morale, etc. His view was to accept all of the issues, but he also reflected that none of it would be fixed without fixing the organization's leadership and culture. The outcome was he gave me 12–18 months and a great HR team to rebuild the organization, attract the right people, pay them well, and get them integrated into the corporate culture and business. If we did that, then *they* would fix all of these other problems. He told the senior team "we" need to embrace this group and encourage them instead of beating up on them all of the time. He stressed that the IT group needed to become an integral part of "our" team if "we" were to be a successful company going forward. That took about 15–20 minutes.

Needless to say, the Nolan/Norton team got their answer about his attention span, and I got the understanding and support I needed. He assigned a top-notch Management Development team of David Hatch, Dan Paxton and Paul Russell to help me rebuild my group. In addition, I was authorized to lease and remodel space in the building and to bring my organization together from a dozen scattered locations. This enabled me to build our culture and pride. And finally, they modernized our pay scales so we could compete for talent from top universities. When Wayne saw what our salary structure was, his reaction was "if you pay peanuts, you get monkeys." In other words, fix it.

Within a couple of years we were delivering with consistency and within five years we had won both the Smithsonian and the Carnegie Mellon Award for Technology Innovation for our implementation of the handheld computer for our 10,000 route salesmen.

Good leaders like Wayne, Mike, and Bill were always available. If any one of us needed to talk to Wayne, we could get to him within 24 hours, either physically or by phone, and if not during the workday, then in the evening or over the weekend. As Steve Reinemund recalled:

> Wayne almost never called me. But I could call him anytime, and if I was going to see him in his office, he never kept me waiting. Whatever reason I was calling for advice, he was always available for me. But he always found the right balance. He never intruded. He never overstepped. He never did anything to take away my own authority and leadership.[9]

The culture of availability radiated through the entire leadership team. You were encouraged to not bury the issues, but you were also expected to bring not only the problem but offer potential solutions.

I remember an early conversation that I had with Wayne soon

after joining PepsiCo. I was embarking upon a critical project that would involve the widespread adoption of an important new technology, a handheld device that would improve tracking and product delivery services at Frito-Lay.

I asked Wayne which would he consider to be a victory: If I promised to accomplish the objective within 36 months, but my team got it done in 35, or if I promised completion in 24 months but the project ended up taking 27. Wayne's response was a model of clarity. He told me that 27 months would be the victory, but only if I reached out to him as soon as I realized that I wouldn't be meeting the 24-month deadline.

As he explained to me, if I told him about problems, we could work together to figure out a solution. Maybe I would need more people to get the job done. Or maybe the rollout of the new technology would have turned out to be so complicated that I needed more time. The important thing would be not to hide any problems that cropped up along the way; we needed to work together to get the job done.

In her 2014 interview for this book, Peggy Moore, who worked with Wayne for many years in roles that included Vice President of Investor Relations, pointed out that he was committed to this approach from his earliest days at PepsiCo. She shared some memories of her first experiences working with him as a recent college graduate, back in 1974, during the period before he was transferred to Frito-Lay's leadership team:

> As a young planning person, I was invited to sit in on some meetings and I would ask myself, "How come Wayne is so important?" He sits in meetings and he doesn't say anything. When he does say something, he usually repeats what people

say.

Years later, I worked with him again, and by that time I had the experience and understanding to appreciate what he would do in those meetings. People who were senior would always know exactly what he was trying to convey by what he would choose to repeat and how he repeated it. If there were a problem, they would understand what the problem was.

He had ways of giving you feedback, even in a group setting, without ever embarrassing you. When I was very young, I didn't understand that, but later on, I appreciated what a tremendous skill that was. Meetings with Wayne were so even-keeled and so effective. As a result of all this, people totally trusted him. They confided in him. They wouldn't be afraid to tell him what was going on.[10]

To those of us who worked with Wayne Calloway and grew up in PepsiCo, that kind of trusting, constructive, forward-looking, problem-solving, get-the-job-done approach became part of our DNA, and it has remained there. It's what has inspired and motivated us throughout our careers and our personal lives.

Another approach that kept us all grounded in reality was the annual requirement that we work on a sales route, at a plant, or at a distribution center. The operative word was "work." Getting up at 3:00 AM on a rainy day, inventorying a route truck in east Texas, and then riding along on that truck to make stops at 20 stores to sell and replenish products—it all gives you a different appreciation of "reality" than sitting in a sales review meeting in the Board Room.

As Peggy Moore recalled:

Back when Wayne was at Frito-Lay, he really helped the

organization to develop the humility to realize you can't mechanize everything. Machines aren't perfect all the time. There's an art element to all this. He was completely committed to the importance of respecting what the guy who operates the production line has to say, because he probably does know better than anyone else.

There was one time when a plant in Canada had a problem: When you looked at all the charts and the numbers, it seemed as though the product would be perfect, but when we actually evaluated it, it wasn't. So Wayne brought in the line guy, who told us, "This line is going down for maintenance pretty soon, and when it gets to this stage, the line runs hot." Those were the kind of nuances that Wayne taught us to look for—and it was because he knew how to listen and reflect and to trust people that this would happen.[11]

Roger King, who served in a number of Human Resource leadership roles, including as Vice President of Labor Relations at Frito-Lay, and ultimately Senior Vice President of Human Resources at PepsiCo, recalled:

When he would go on plant tours, he would take time to listen to all of the presentations that the various supervisors had put together, which could be quite tedious and time consuming. Once while driving back to the plane someone on the tour complained that they had heard that same presentation 3-4 times, and Wayne said, "So have I, but I wanted to make sure he knew how important what he does is to this company."[12]

At PepsiCo, these shared experiences were part of the rhythm and dialogue that led to innovative thinking and a different type of problem solving. Our goal was to get the stretch growth that the agenda called for. But the path was often circuitous and littered with problems we had to solve together along the way. How we solved the problems was left to us, but you could get all the help you needed because of the open culture that was created and nurtured throughout the corporation.

There's one more reason that leaders don't drill down deeply into the details of the current situation, which is that they don't think it's their job. Their job is to set the overall strategy. Everyone else's job is to deal with details and concentrate on execution.

Remember the earlier discussion of the "either/or" approach? For those leaders, their telescopes are basically stuck on the long-term perspective. Because they don't understand that successfully setting an agenda depends upon the "and/and" perspective, they think that they can accomplish their goals and achieve whatever is on their leadership agenda by simply creating a compelling vision of the future state.

As a management strategy, this is shortsighted and incomplete. Leaders whose "lens" is only focused on the distant horizon assume that if everyone knew where they were all (hopefully) heading, they would get excited and motivated, quickly lining up and racing to get there—that is, to the place in the future at which all goals would be accomplished and all necessary change would inevitably have happened.

The fallacy with this approach, however, is that if everyone has a different starting point or different frame of reference relating to the current state, and a different understanding of the root causes of whatever current conditions may exist, then they will each attack the journey from a different angle and intensity. They won't work together and align toward a common vision and plan. This problem is compounded by the inevitable domino effect, as different groups continue to repeat the same pattern.

Why do I use the image of "attacking the journey"? I choose the word "attack" carefully, because it conveys the chaos that can and usually does ensue when everyone begins the journey by starting from a different angle and intensity, causing collisions and conflicts.

For Wayne Calloway, whose "lens" was clear and focused on both the current state and the future state, avoiding this was fairly straightforward. Setting the agenda depended upon, first, establishing the current state (in other words, coming to an understanding and articulation of reality). The next step was to formulate, and then communicate, a compelling vision of the future state—where we wanted to get.

Here again, it's remarkable how relatively few leaders and organizations do this well. They might tackle pieces of the challenge, perhaps by commissioning strategy studies or comprehensive reports from consulting firms such as McKinsey, Boston Consulting Group (BCG), or Bain & Company. In many cases, the executive team and board of directors might even move matters along to the next stage by signing off on some key recommendations and allocating resources to begin the process of changing from current to future state. They might embark upon a major M&A program, massive product or services innovations, a comprehensive IT upgrade, significant productivity initiatives, or geographic expansion, or even have adopted some components of all these.

But the end results fail to achieve target objectives, and therefore fall short of what was once envisioned. That's because very few organizations or leaders seek to integrate the various components of change into a fabric that has a higher purpose than any individual component and then articulate it in a way that constituents can consume. On the other hand, when this is accomplished, it motivates people and institutions to align towards that inspiring vision of the future and to work together to achieve the larger goals.

Wayne was a master at all this. Through the example he set, and the reinforcement that managers received at all levels of the organization through PepsiCo's highly effective "Leadership Development" system, the men and women we worked with at PepsiCo knew how to accomplish this for their teams as well.

Throughout my career, I have tried to pass these influential lessons and insights along to others who face challenges getting from the current to the future state, whether in businesses or other types of institutions.

People long for a leader who inspires them. They want someone who gives them a sense of purpose and belonging while also helping them understand why what they're doing matters. That's true for corporations, other institutions, and societies as a whole.

Wayne's skill at setting the agenda at PepsiCo helped accomplish this for men and women throughout the organization. Interestingly enough, he was far from the kind of public speaker who we might think of as passionate or fiery. But at the end of the day, what mattered most was substance. People responded to his compelling ideas.

What came across when Wayne communicated with people throughout the organization were his values, his priorities and commitment, and a clear vision of what he thought of and expected from everyone who was a part of the PepsiCo community. It wasn't about him or anyone else trying to pretend that they were superhuman. It was about having us all join together as a team that was completely aligned according to the agenda that he established.

As Steve Reinemund describes it:

> Wayne was a man who managed to combine strong leadership and a deeply competitive spirit with a sense of selflessness. He loved to win as a team sport—and he was much more interested in the team winning than in himself being a star. He took pride and gratification from making other people successful, rather than ever looking to applaud himself for having some brilliant strategy. It was all about the team doing the absolute best that it could do.[13]

Ironically enough, for a man who was always more comfortable listening to others than talking, Wayne appreciated that it was the role of a leader to not only set the agenda but to communicate about it, and to do so in ways that would help PepsiCo's key constituents to understand and embrace it. As a result, when it came to PepsiCo's strong growth agenda, Wayne reiterated this message with absolute clarity, commitment, and consistency, both inside and outside the organization.

So, for example, in an "Experiencing PepsiCo" speech that he delivered to employees in May 1995, he sketched out an exciting prospect of the future state, even while acknowledging some of the challenges that they would all need to work together to confront:

> Think about an extraordinary portfolio of powerful brands, gigantic markets that span the globe, and literally billions of consumers that haven't yet had their first taste of what we have to offer. Think about bright, creative people like you, with the

freedom and resources to drive growth wherever there's a great opportunity. You see, we really do believe PepsiCo's sales can grow…even though nobody needs our products, consumer tastes are changing, and our competitors are among the toughest in the world.

There are many elements involved in successfully establishing the leadership agenda, but one key aspect of this is the ability to articulate future goals and help people understand the ways that various initiatives or actions fit together to help the corporation or institution make the journey to the desirable future state.

Here's a good example of what this means. An organization might be pursuing a number of objectives: increase productivity, encourage innovation, and achieve expansion goals by adding products and services, carrying out M&A activities, and moving into new geographic regions. By presenting the cohesive story that unites all of these together, a strong and effective leader would move from a realistic assessment of the current challenges to a clear expression of what's possible, and along the way articulate how all these various elements help support the achievement of these objectives. By doing so, such a leader would increase the odds of alignment, thereby creating a huge tailwind that would help make change happen.

In contrast, a weak leader might launch a gaggle of initiatives, creating a corporate environment in which employees and managers alike feel as if they've been hit by a contradictory and complex to-do list. Because each initiative seems isolated, individuals throughout the corporation have trouble understanding the way that each program can actually be connected to a coherent whole, with all of these aligning to the overall agenda and the long-term goal of reaching the future state.

In such situations, conditions are frightening, confusing, and unpredictable. Employees and managers find themselves feeling as though nothing makes sense, because they don't understand the overall context of current and future state. In this situation, the leader might produce "crosswinds," "headwinds," and "tailwinds," ending up with people throughout the organization moving in all kinds of directions and at cross-purposes because there's nothing powerful that can align them in the same direction.

In today's business world, time and "fuel" are both scarce commodities. Great leaders know how to put "the wind" behind them and make it work in their favor. A dual lens—an "and/and" approach to setting the agenda that strategically engages with both the current state and the future state—is a key component in making this happen.

* * *

Wayne Calloway was the type of leader who brought cohesion and a strong sense of meaning. This was incredibly valuable given the huge number of initiatives we had going on in pursuit of our growth strategy. Some might question whether he would have been as successful with his leadership approach today as he was during the '70s, '80s, and '90s. They might argue that managing change is more difficult for businesses, public entities, and other institutions, such as universities and hospitals, during the turbulent 21st century than has ever been the case. They might think of the decades during which Wayne led Frito-Lay and then PepsiCo as ancient history.

It might seem at first glance as though I would agree with such readers. After all, I began this book by describing the ways the technology-driven change is now taking place at a more rapid pace and with a broader and more immediate impact than ever before. As I noted, Moore's Law implies that these forces will continue to gain momentum in the years to come, with new technologies inevitably forcing us to deal with change unlike anything we've ever experienced. I argued that this was at the core of our current crisis in leadership and our pressing need for a renaissance in leadership.

But, in fact, my position here strongly supports the timeless value of the Calloway Leadership Model, as tested and proven over decades at PepsiCo. It was designed to help a huge and successful corporation *continuously* and aggressively change in order to get better and better.

In fact, this leadership model achieved all that it did during an era in which there was less "wind" (in other words, significant less overall momentum for change) than we're now experiencing in the 21st century. That means it was even harder to aggressively drive growth, change, and innovation. When conditions are good, it's all too easy for organizations and their leaders to become complacent.

One point worth emphasizing is that Calloway—and, in fact, the entire organization that he led during those 25 years of corporate transformation—was deeply forward-looking. In many ways, the strategic dialogue that went on between leaders and their teams throughout the ranks at PepsiCo could have taken place just as easily today as they did during the 1970s, '80s, and '90s. I would argue that this was one important measure of what made this company, and the generation of leaders that it produced, great.

It's difficult, for example, to believe that it was nearly 20 years ago that he offered these insights to the H.W. Lay Leadership Forum:

There are different segments of the public doing different things, sending very contradictory messages. And as our world continues to grow in freedom and opportunity, this will continue for sure. There will be more signals and they will be harder to read. That tells me we have to do two things: even more research and study of the marketplace, combined with even more personal, world-wise insights. And we have to be out there trying lots of things—constantly.

One of Wayne Calloway's big management themes was, "If it ain't broke, fix it anyway; if you don't, your competitors will!"

As Peggy Moore recalled:

Back then, a lot of people would have taken the attitude, if it's working well, why not stay with it? But Wayne understood, change is inevitable. You've got to be ready and poised for change.

This was "pre-"everything that we're now experiencing be-cause of the impact of digital technologies. He understood, an organization could be at the top of the heap today and then suddenly something could change and it would be unable to compete. He never let us rest on our laurels, and he took every competitor very seriously.[14]

This proactive mindset defined his approach when it came to setting the agenda, and it was instilled in leaders throughout the corporation. It demonstrated its value in many ways during the Calloway era at PepsiCo, and I believe it holds great value for us, both now and in the future.

* * *

An "Experiencing PepsiCo" speech that Wayne delivered in April 1995 still seems contemporary today, offering a management perspective that resonates just as strongly in 2014 as it did for his audience 20 years ago. In this speech, he made a strong connection between PepsiCo's growth-focused agenda and its corporate history: stressing the four key values that were at the center of the corporation—passion for growth, high standards, innovation, and integrity:

> To me, the first thing is a huge passion for growth. All of [PepsiCo's] early leaders were extremely ambitious, looking to grow in dramatic ways. Herman Lay didn't want to own a snack food company, he wanted to own every snack food company in America—and a few soft drink companies, too. The Carney brothers had an idea for a pizza restaurant[15] while they were in college. And before spring break, they had begun awarding franchises to their college buddies. Picture it. Two guys from Wichita who didn't know the difference between pepperoni and Parmesan, and they're launching Italian restaurants across America. That's ambition. They weren't interested in running Mom and Pop operations. They wanted to be part of something very big and very special.
>
> To me, the perfect symbol for all of this is right here—PepsiCo's headquarters. People with small dreams don't build wonderful buildings like this. Don Kendall and Herman Lay, our founders, wanted a great and extraordinary corporation and they went for it.

At a January 1995 speech before the Pepsi-Cola Bottlers, he

told them:

> For 30 years, we've billed ourselves as a growth company. So
> we work relentlessly to grow, to develop, to change, to expand,
> to create new things, to find new ways, to come up with new
> ideas.

And here's how he described the corporation's growth agenda
at a September 1995 meeting with a crucial external audience, investment analysts:

> By relentlessly focusing on our key growth performance mea-
> sures—volume, operating profit, and cash flow—and invest-
> ment returns, PepsiCo has become a stronger company. Better
> yet, PepsiCo is well positioned to capture the opportunities of
> our enormous marketplace, which is over a half-trillion dol-
> lars and growing. Finally, our results demonstrate that a com-
> pany dedicated to innovation has boundless potential. Each
> year, a big part of our sales growth comes from new things we
> do, like new products, new packages, and new ways of distrib-
> uting our products.

Leaders who are successful in communicating the core themes
of their agendas recognize that the effort to build understanding
and alignment needs to be multifaceted and consistent over time.
At PepsiCo, Wayne may have started the drumbeat, but it was up
to each and every leader throughout the organization to consistently repeat it to his or her team.

One way that Wayne achieved this was by repeatedly articulat-
ing to men and women throughout the corporation the message
that growth was fundamental to PepsiCo's mission—and their

own. What better way to unify employees around the growth agenda than to help people understand their personal as well as the corporate connection to this agenda. So, for example, at a Mars/Hostess/Frito-Lay Luncheon in July 1994, he emphasized:

> Growth is what builds teamwork. It's what drives creativity. It's what satisfies your career ambitions and your personal needs.... And what happens if we stop growing? Well, the demands for growth might be rigorous, but the effect of not growing is rigor mortis. It's deadly for the spirit. Without growth, there's no opportunity for ambitious people. Nowhere to go. The environment becomes political with everybody fighting for a bigger slice of a pie that isn't getting any bigger.

As Joe McCann, who worked with Wayne both at Frito-Lay and at PepsiCo in leading corporate communications roles, put it:

> There was a simplicity and clarity about the message. Wayne never said very much, but everyone understood this: growth was key. It was 100% important. This started with Don Kendall and Andy Pearson, but they were the ones who hired Wayne and chose him as the leadership successor. He embodied it. He never wavered on this. Growth was the goal.[16]

* * *

If great leadership begins with setting the agenda, the true test is whether it delivers results with consistency. In this next chapter, we will examine in detail the way that the Calloway Leadership Model achieved this at PepsiCo over the course of 25 years.

Exceptionally strong and consistent results were achieved,

despite a wide range of competitive, economic, and other external challenges. And that was the case, in large part, because people throughout the institution understood the agenda and were aligned with it. Importantly, they were encouraged to take appropriate risks, in order to achieve target results. Thanks to the clarity that Wayne Calloway provided, we kept our own "telescopes" focused on both the near- and long-term horizons.

Unfortunately, there are all too many good leaders who find their time cut short because they fail to deliver results quickly and consistently enough to satisfy directors and shareholders. There may be any number of root problems. The leader might not, perhaps, have done a good enough job of conveying to the team that achieving short-term goals needs to be a given, no matter how focused they all might be on achieving the future state. At PepsiCo, that's one mistake Wayne never made. His simple drumbeat was "Results and Integrity."

Whether he was at the helm of Frito-Lay or PepsiCo, Wayne Calloway consistently managed to achieve against the aggressive targets in his short- and long-term leadership agenda. Year after year, he and the world-class organization he led consistently delivered great results for shareholders, with growth that outpaced the market and improved profit margins.

Let's turn, now, to chapter 3 for a more detailed examination of the way that Calloway's Leadership model did such a successful job of "Delivering With Consistency."

NOTES

1. Donald R. Keough, qtd. in: Constance L. Hays, "Wayne Calloway Dies at 62; Was Chief at PepsiCo 10 Years," The New York Times, July 10, 1998.

2. Steve Reinemund, Interview, 2014.

3. Indra K. Nooyi, Interview, 2014.

4. Joe McCann, Interview, 2014.

5. Ibid.

6. Bill Bensyl, Interview, 2014.

7. Roger King, Interview, 2014.

8. Tom Peters, Interview, 2014.

9. Steve Reinemund, Interview, 2014.

10. Peggy Moore, Interview, 2014.

11. Ibid.

12. Roger King, Interview, 2014.

13. Steve Reinemund, Interview, 2014.

14. Peggy Moore, Interview, 2014.

15. Pizza Hut was founded in 1958 by brothers Dan and Frank Carney in Wichita, Kansas. http://www.pizzahut-me.com/our-story.

16. 16. Joe McCann, Interview, 2014.

June 8, 1988 | Wayne Calloway playing golf at the Manufacturers Hanover Pro-Am Golf Classic at the Westchester Club at 52 years old. His partner was Greg Norman.

November 11, 1987 | Wayne Calloway, Executive-in-Residence at The Center for Entrepreneurship at Wichita State University with Dan and Frank Carney, the founders of Pizza Hut, and Steve Reinemund.

November 12, 1991 | Lou Gerstner, President George H.W. Bush, and Wayne Calloway at the New York fundraiser to re-elect Bush.

November 12, 1991 | Wayne Calloway standing with George H.W. and Barbara Bush.

April 15, 1988 | President Ronald Reagan greets Wayne Calloway at the Vote America Luncheon at the White House.

Wayne and his wife, Jan, at the General Electric Senior Management and Board of Directors Christmas Party at the Rainbow Room in New York City.

June 9, 1995 | Wayne Calloway contemplating his putt at the Blind Brook Club.

March, 1992 | (left to right, top row) June Schorr, Jan Calloway, Chuck & Toni Peebler, (bottom row) Paul Schorr, and Wayne Calloway in Snowmass, Colorado.

February 14, 1995 | (left to right) Paul & June Schorr, Chuck Peebler, Bim Kendall, Toni Peebler, Don Kendall, Jan & Wayne Calloway, Joe McCann, and Karen & Grant Gregory standing in front of Calloway Hall on Founder's Day.

February 4, 1986 | Wayne Calloway with Betty Ford at the Founder's Day Luncheon at Wake Forest University where he received the Merit of Honor Award.

February 4, 1986 | Bones McKinney, former basketball coach for Calloway, greets him at the Wake Forest University Founder's Day Luncheon.

September 12, 1992 | Wayne Calloway on his 57th birthday, enjoying his gift from Jan Calloway.

CHAPTER THREE
DELIVERING WITH CONSISTENCY

"DELIVERING WITH CONSISTENCY" is an essential aspect of great leadership. To state what *should* be obvious, if a leader fails to deliver results consistently, he has failed. Great leaders think big, aim high, and inspire others to achieve a shared agenda that is meaningful.

Great leaders have the courage to accept personal responsibility and accountability in their role as the face of the organization. Then, as they set the institutional agenda, they encourage and expect accountability and responsibility from their leaders—throughout the organization—in alignment with the short and longer-term strategic objectives inherent in that agenda.

Wayne Calloway embodied this model of leadership, and he never shied away from personal accountability. It's interesting to consider the way that business observers recognized this back when he was running PepsiCo. For example, in January 1992, during a period when the corporation was confronting a number of difficult challenges, *Business Week* published an article titled, "Can Wayne Calloway Handle the PepsiCo Challenge?"[1]

The reporter quoted the CEO as saying, "We have consciously and deliberately created a corporate culture that sanctions individual power." She then concluded, "If his strategy unleashes chaos, Calloway will have to answer for it. If it works, he can credit the employees."[2]

As history went on to prove, the result of Calloway's leadership model was anything but chaotic. I would argue, however, that this reporter was wrong. For all the credit that PepsiCo's employees deserve for the corporation's long track record of success during this period, Wayne Calloway and his leadership model deserve credit as well.

* * *

Calloway joined PepsiCo in 1967. From 1970 to 1983, he rose within the Frito-Lay organization, assuming its leadership in 1976. In all, he helped drive more than a decade of unprecedented growth for Frito-Lay. During this era, Frito-Lay transitioned from a strong regional company to a national snack food powerhouse. The snack foods division's operating profits tripled over the course of the seven years he spent at its helm.[3]

In 1983, Wayne Calloway moved from the Frito-Lay headquarters in Plano, Texas to the PepsiCo headquarters in Purchase, New York, first stepping into the role of CFO. There he went on to take the reins of the company in 1986 as Chairman and Chief Executive, until his retirement in 1996. This was an era of transformation and accomplishment for PepsiCo, during which the corporation developed from its position as a major, but mostly domestic, consumer goods corporation into a truly global consumer giant. Under his direction, PepsiCo's market value increased by

$35 billion.[4]

As described in the previous chapter, Wayne's agenda was always about growth. And he delivered on that agenda. Throughout the span of Calloway's leadership, both Frito-Lay and its parent, PepsiCo, achieved impressive growth with remarkable consistency. During this period, Frito-Lay and PepsiCo performed exceptionally on a year-to-year basis, typically growing at a rate that not only beat the market but also almost always met the double-digit growth rate enshrined as the "PepsiCo Standard."

That record was well appreciated during the years Calloway spent at PepsiCo's helm. During his remarks at a September 1995 Analyst Meeting, for example, the CEO cited a report that had recently appeared in *Fortune* magazine, noting that, "Of all the companies in the original Fortune 500, the one with the single highest growth rate since 1954 is PepsiCo."

Wayne pointed out in one of his speeches that the *Fortune* study highlighted a growth trajectory that spanned four decades. So it is worth pointing out that this record was achieved thanks to the efforts of a number of strong and successful PepsiCo executives, including cofounder and long-time CEO Don Kendall, former PepsiCo President Andy Pearson, and Harold Lilley, the former chief executive of Frito-Lay. Yet Wayne Calloway deserves to be singled out for the leadership role he played in institutionalizing the PepsiCo growth agenda and for helping the corporation maintain its entrepreneurial spirit and fast-growth momentum, even as it developed into a global giant.

To get a good sense of the growth that was achieved during the Calloway years, consider the CEO's remarks at a Mars/Hostess/Frito-Lay Luncheon that took place in July 1994. He noted:

In 1978, total sales at PepsiCo were about $4 billion. Today, nearly every one of our division presidents runs a company worth more than all of PepsiCo a decade and a half ago. That, my friends, is the happy result of growth. More opportunity. More responsibility. More diversity. All the things that keep organizations grand and glorious, vital, and vigorous.

Whether in a roomful of PepsiCo employees or in a speech before a large public audience, Calloway often highlighted statistics that demonstrated PepsiCo's outstanding growth record. At a PepsiCo Personnel Conference held in Phoenix, Arizona in April 1994, he told the group:

> You remember the old saying, "You'd better watch what you wish for, because you may just get it." Well, at PepsiCo we wished for growth. And worked awfully hard for it. Today, we're the 15th largest industrial company in the U.S. and something like the 50th in the world. And at the rate we're growing, we're creating the equivalent of a Fortune 300 company every four months. Every year, our growth amounts to a company the size of The Hershey Company, Casio Computer, or De Beers Mining…
>
> When you look at what our own growth as a business means in terms of people, it's almost staggering. With 423,000 employees, we're already the fifth-largest corporate employer in the world.

The next year, in a May 1995 "Experiencing PepsiCo" speech, he mused about "PepsiCo's special qualities—what it's taken for us to double in size about every five years for a quarter century." And, in fact, by 1995, the last full year during which Wayne Calloway led PepsiCo, the corporation's sales had climbed to just over $30 billion.[5] Notably, about $7.8 billion of that came from international sales,[6] an area that Calloway had consistently prioritized because of what he recognized as its high-growth potential. In fact, by 1996, international sales were experiencing a compounded annual growth rate of 20% annually over the previous five years.[7]

By any measure of growth, PepsiCo's results were outstanding. During the period from 1990–95, the beverage division grew at a compounded annual growth rate of 10%. Although the U.S. growth rate within the division was 7%, international growth was at a compounded annual average of 19%. Within snack foods, the five-year average was 10% growth, with international growth at a compounded annual rate of 19%, which added up to a five-year annual growth rate of 12%. Meanwhile, within the restaurant division, the U.S. compounded annual rate for this period was 11%, with international growth at a whopping 25%, bringing the division's compounded annual growth rate to 13%.

Overall, during the 1990–95 period, PepsiCo's combined U.S. segments grew by 9%, international grew by 20% annually, and revenue for the corporation as a whole was up by 12% on a compounded annual basis. During this same period, the corporation's operating profit increased by 11% annually.[9]

Taking an even longer-term perspective, if one considers the period from 1986 through 1996, PepsiCo's net sales grew at a compounded annual rate of 13%, while operating income increased by 12% annually, and net income rose by 10%. Meanwhile, at the beginning of this period, PepsiCo had 214,000 employees. Ten years later, the number had more than doubled, to 486,000 men and women working for the corporation worldwide.[10]

This is not to say, of course, that PepsiCo did not face its fair share of challenges. There were some years when results fell short. 1996, the year in which Calloway stepped down, was a particularly difficult year, during which Pepsi-Cola's international business experienced significant losses, requiring major restructuring of the corporation.

Yet what remains remarkable about Frito-Lay's and PepsiCo's performance during the Calloway era was the overall consistency of strong results over such an extended period of time. PepsiCo truly was a growth machine. For today's readers, who might lack the historical context, the assumption might be that growth was "easier" to achieve back then, because it was a "kinder, gentler" time when the American economy was strong, global competition was scarce, and promising opportunities were scattered across the horizon, just waiting for corporations to seize them.

In fact, the Calloway years were marked by a number of serious economic and business challenges. These included three U.S. economic recessions: the 1974–75 downturn that followed the 1973 oil crisis and collapse of the Bretton Woods monetary system; the early 1980s recession, which came on the heels of the 1979 energy crisis; and the early 1990s recession, which was followed by a so-called jobless recovery.

In contrast to the first couple of decades that followed World War II, the 1970s, when Wayne Calloway first joined PepsiCo, were a time marked by weak consumer confidence and prolonged problems for the U.S. at home and abroad, including high energy prices and oil shortages, which hit corporations and families alike. With odd or even days determining when families could line up to fill the tanks of their cars, and businesses like Frito-Lay watching their transportation costs go sky high, inflation was rampant and financial pressures abounded. Meanwhile, although the Reagan years helped usher in the new confidence of a "morning in America," the 1980s also witnessed a savings and loan crisis and widespread bank failures, and then, in 1987, the stock market crash known as Black Monday.

Meanwhile, to all those who might assume that competition in the good old days was just a shadow of what corporations must grapple with these days, I would point to the "Cola Wars." Although they had long been the fiercest of rivals, PepsiCo and Coca-Cola gained legendary status in the world of advertising and marketing (as well as in many consumers' memories) when they started explicitly targeting each other's products in commercials. The opening salvo was 1975's Pepsi Challenge, in which consumers who took a blind taste test showed a definite preference for Pepsi over Coke. Pepsi's market share climbed during the next decade. But although Coca-Cola made some major blunders, most notably the launch of New Coke, the competitive environment remained fierce throughout the Calloway years—and not only on the beverage front.

In 1995, Wayne Calloway's last full year in office, PepsiCo's Annual Report described the competition the corporation faced in a way that fully conveys just how tough this environment then was. (While the specific details differed year to year, the general picture could have described PepsiCo's competitive environment throughout Wayne Calloway's more than 25-year career within the organization.)

It read:

All of PepsiCo's businesses are highly competitive. PepsiCo's beverages and snack foods compete in the United States and internationally with widely distributed products of a number

of major companies that have plants in many of the areas PepsiCo serves, as well as with private label soft drinks and snack
foods and with the products of local and regional manufac-
turers.

As the Annual Report continued to disclose:

PepsiCo's restaurants compete in the United States and internationally with other restaurants, restaurant chains, food
outlets and home delivery operations. PFS competes in the
United States and internationally with other food distribution
companies. For all of PepsiCo's industry segments, the main
areas of competition are price, quality, variety of products, and
customer service.[11]

Or, as Wayne himself put it in the "Experiencing PepsiCo"
speech quoted earlier that he delivered to employees in May 1995,
"nobody *needs* our products, consumer tastes are changing, and
our competitors are among the toughest in the world." How's that
for tough?

* * *

Delivering with consistency is difficult, and it is a relatively rare
accomplishment for any organization to achieve, especially over
time. In the case of PepsiCo during this period, a number of key
elements played important roles in helping the organization to
achieve this.

Having a clear and appropriate agenda is absolutely essential.
So is institution-wide resilience, staying power, and a firm sense
of balance. In PepsiCo's case, the commitment to excellence and

innovation were also invaluable. As a leader, Wayne provided the vision and support to make all this happen.

An early experience in Calloway's career at Frito-Lay provides a good example of what resilience and staying power meant to him. This experience is also revealing in terms of the way he viewed these to both be core attributes of the PepsiCo organization. Here's how he recalled it during the "Experiencing PepsiCo" speech he gave in May 1995:

> Once when I was working at Frito-Lay for Harold Lilley, we had a lot of pressure from supermarkets in California to change our method of delivery. We were taking our products in through the front of the store and putting them on the racks ourselves. But a few of the major supermarket chains wanted us to deliver our products to the storeroom in the back.
>
> California was one of Frito's biggest markets, so we debated this for some time. There was product freshness to consider, and the appearance of our displays. Ultimately, we decided not to comply with their request. It was store-door delivery—or nothing. Well, the supermarkets threw us out of their stores.
>
> Imagine if you will what it must have been like for Harold Lilley to walk into Don Kendall's office and tell him what had happened. We weren't going to make our numbers that quarter. Our bonuses were going to suffer. Our market share was going to drop off the charts.
>
> But, you know something? Don supported the decision. So did everyone else, right down to the sales people and route truck drivers. Everyone knew that back-door delivery was wrong for the business. And we stuck to our guns. It turns out our competitors had a couple of wonderful quarters. But six

months later, it became pretty clear that consumers wanted Frito-Lay products. We made the right decision. But I can tell you there were some pretty tense moments.

The point is, integrity means all sorts of things at PepsiCo. But a big part of it is having a clear vision of what you think is right. That doesn't mean being closed-minded or headstrong. It does mean sticking to high standards of quality, and high standards of behavior. And it means making decisions that are right for the business in the long-term, despite the short-term pain.

All of us who worked closely with Wayne saw how powerfully he embodied that same conviction and resilience. Joe McCann recalled:

Wayne had a remarkable ability to live with uncertainty. Most CEOs can't do that—they have to control everything. But he had a belief that what you had to do was focus on growth-oriented businesses and find the right people to run them. But then, you had to be prepared to give the managers the freedom to do what they wanted to do. As he would say, if you have eagles, you need to let them fly. It was his job to keep them flying in formation.[12]

Throughout Wayne's career, he consistently aimed to encourage bold ideas, informed risk-taking, and always a focus on aggressive growth by ensuring that leaders throughout the organization recognized and appreciated PepsiCo's strength and staying power. As a leader, he didn't second-guess them; instead, he focused on encouraging and empowering them.

Meanwhile, he used his leadership role to reinforce at all times

PepsiCo's commitment to, and expertise at, innovation, which he believed was at the core of the corporation's extraordinary success. As he put it at a June 1995 Security Analyst Meeting:

> Some people think innovation is the domain of high-tech companies and that's one reason they have a big future. But I believe there's as much innovation in a potato chip as a computer chip, especially if that potato chip comes from PepsiCo… In my opinion, PepsiCo demonstrates year after year, year in and year out, that we are the most innovative package goods company on earth in terms of new products, packages, and systems.
>
> This is extremely important for a consumer company, because innovation is a matter of discipline, not luck. Our system is geared to innovation and we do it with relatively little risk and almost boring regularity—well, not so boring to me, actually…
>
> [For example, we] tinkered innovatively with an unheralded product line at Frito-Lay and made it a $300 million product. I'm talking about the modest Rold Gold Pretzel.
>
> And for PepsiCo, Rold Gold was only one product in one division that had many other innovations. And that division was only one in a company full of innovative divisions. For example, in soft drinks, the cube package sells at the rate of 400 a minute today. That's 24,000 an hour, 600,000 a day, 200,000,000 a year. And the cube didn't even exist two years ago.

There are countless stories, far too numerous to detail, that illustrate the way that the Calloway Leadership model encouraged the delivery of exceptional results, year after year, through a corporate culture and set of systems built upon resilience, staying power, innovation, and more. Without attempting to be fully comprehensive, it is useful to examine the way that the growth-oriented agenda got translated into some specific initiatives in ways that led to results that were strong and consistent, regardless of whatever challenges were posed by the economy, corporate competitors, regulators, and other forces.

* * *

A good place to pick up the story is in 1978, the first year when food products (the Frito-Lay division) posted \$1 billion in revenues, up 18% from the previous year. Operating profits rose by 36% during this same period.[13] All this was achieved despite a troubled economy, high unemployment rates, and a host of other U.S. economic woes that could well have stymied the PepsiCo growth agenda.

There were three strategic efforts that combined to drive impressive growth in sales, market share, and profitability over both the short- *and* the long-term:

1. successful innovation in new product lines

2. highly effective marketing of existing brands

3. improved operational efficiency and capacity

More specifically, during this time, a handful of new product lines were introduced, including nacho cheese Cheetos and BBQ Ruffles, that are still on the market today. Meanwhile, fresh new advertising and marketing campaigns invigorated the sales of many of the existing products and brands.

During 1979, Frito-Lay added 900 domestic sales routes,

boosting its store-door network to over 8,000 points of sale. Thanks to increased efficiencies, Frito-Lay was able to keep its costs relatively level, despite a fuel crisis and vehicle-related expenses. Adjustments such as the introduction of larger bags helped improve sales tonnage and boost domestic unit volume by 11% in 1979, as operating profits rose by 13%.[14]

By 1980, Frito-Lay was the largest profit center within Pepsi-Co's three core businesses. Despite the still-floundering U.S. economy, Frito doubled down on its growth agenda, beginning with the construction of 30 new distribution centers and increasing its sales force by 10%, all in a bid to aggressively expand and grab market share.[15] It was an emblematic Wayne Calloway move: by delivering exceptional short-term results—built upon a foundation of innovative strategies, strong sales, and controlled costs—he positioned the organization to make large capital investments and take some gutsy risks in pursuit of robust future growth.

The commitment to operational excellence was a core theme throughout the Calloway era, and there are countless examples of how he used strategic initiatives to deliver results on this front. During his years at Frito-Lay, for example, this commitment, combined with his vision of aggressive long-term growth, led him to consistently invest in new, largely unknown technologies in the interest of saving time, reducing space requirements, achieving cost reductions, and improving the quality of Frito-Lay products. These numerous initiatives were typically "bundled" in multi-year named programs such as "Double in Place." By setting a huge stretch "theme," this encouraged and allowed us to develop both large and small projects that would deliver the overall program's agenda.

Significantly, between 1975 and 1981, Frito-Lay plants doubled their output capacity per hour.[16] By 1983, they significantly increased the volume of finished product per pound of raw material by implementing technologies like computerized scales to more accurately weigh products.[17]

What really drove Frito-Lay's success during the early years—and throughout the Calloway era at PepsiCo—was the balance between improving existing operations to deliver immediate results and investing in future growth opportunities to lay the groundwork for long-term success. (The PepsiCo Food products division consisted of Frito-Lay, the domestic giant that Calloway drove, and Pepsi Foods International, which operated in Europe, Canada, and Mexico.)

The international market for snack foods was miniscule back then, but PepsiCo recognized the future growth potential inherent in global expansion and continued to invest in this division despite insignificant profit contributions during these early years. Indeed, in a strategy that Calloway continued to replicate throughout his leadership years, Frito-Lay's exceptional growth and profits helped average out the sub-par international performance while also supporting valuable, although costly, investments in new product research and development, product line extensions, improved packaging, and other steps forward.

These investments in the future paid off in many ways—including as the Food division's focus on international became part of a larger, corporate-wide initiative that spanned all three core businesses and helped make PepsiCo the great global corporation it is today. Indeed, in later years, exceptionally robust international growth rates helped balance out the sometimes slower (on a relative basis, although still impressive) growth in U.S. markets.

When Wayne stepped into the top leadership at PepsiCo in

1983, he first served as the corporation's CFO, a role in which he helped develop and carry out a strategic refocusing of the corporation, which included major divestitures of non-core units. Joe McCann described this period in the following way:

> At the time, we owned a group of companies that included North American Van Lines, Leeway Shipping, and Wilson Sporting Goods. He didn't see how any of them could grow at the same rate as soft drinks, snack foods, and restaurants. In a low-keyed way but with astonishing speed, he divested PepsiCo of them all and clarified the corporation. We were left with three very strong businesses, all with great capacity for growth. From then on, his job was to find the right people to lead them—which he did in spades.[18]

Peggy Moore described the background that helped inform Wayne's approach to refocusing the corporation:

> Before he came to PepsiCo, Wayne had worked at ITT, so he understood conglomerates, and he understood why Pepsi-Co had grown the way it had. But he knew that there wasn't an overriding strategic focus. A lot of people didn't think we could get there back then, but he did. And he was truly instrumental in helping to make that happen—although he would never be one to capture the fanfare.[19]

Despite his pivotal role in this strategic realignment of the corporation, Wayne repeatedly took the opportunity throughout the years to express his gratitude to the leadership team of Don Kendall and Andy Pearson for taking some of the "hits" connected with this restructuring.

This was another defining experience for him in terms of his understanding of the core attributes that contributed to effective leadership. Here's how he described it in the "Experiencing Pepsi-Co" speech from May 1995:

> I'm sure you've all had the experience of going into a new job or a new assignment with high hopes. Your predecessor has built up your expectations. You hear all sorts of promises of excitement, fulfillment, and personal rewards. But after you've been in the job for a while, you begin to realize that things are not quite as rosy as you expected.
>
> You're in your new office on your first day, somebody drops by to welcome you, and casually mentions that your department's about 50% behind plan. Oh, and you've just lost your marketing director. And by the way, there probably won't be a strike *this* week—they've postponed it to next week. I think we've all been through something like this.
>
> Well, ten years ago, I had the exact *opposite* experience. When Don Kendall and Andy Pearson were nearing retirement, and getting ready to hand off leadership of the corporation, they had lots of choices. For example, they could have easily avoided making tough decisions, leaving them for the new kid. They could have invested slightly less and made their own performance look even better. But they didn't. Instead, under their leadership, we sold off businesses that didn't fit our strategic vision. North American Van Lines, for instance, and Leeway. We sold Wilson Sporting Goods. That was a tough one for golfers and tennis buffs. Then there was our problem in the Philippines and Mexico. An executive had cooked the books and we had to take some enormous write-offs. The stock

price was devastated.

They could have abandoned international or taken an easy way out. Instead, they helped refocus and restage our entire international business. They encouraged us to do things that wouldn't pay off until years after they were gone. Don and Andy didn't take the easy way. They continued to manage the company as if it were a startup and they were going to be around for 10 or 20 years. As a result, they made my job a lot easier. We all looked good in those first couple of years.

To me, what Don and Andy did was demonstrate real integrity. It was a lesson for me, and I believe a symbol for what PepsiCo has at its core, the kind of thing we should stand for.

When Calloway stepped into the role of Chairman and CEO in 1986, he had a clear vision for PepsiCo's future that was based on strong, consistent growth and profitability. He—and his leadership team throughout this rapidly growing, increasingly international corporation—made that vision a reality. But it was Wayne, in his new role, who was ultimately accountable for all strategic decisions and establishing this close-knit community that was built upon a culture of competition, winning, pride, integrity, and a feeling of ownership that employees had, whether they were store-door salesmen or home office executives. And he accomplished all this while transforming PepsiCo from a domestic consumer goods powerhouse into a global giant.

Calloway's impact on PepsiCo was felt immediately. While the primary goal in his earlier years as CEO was to take PepsiCo's international presence to the next level, he focused his efforts throughout the corporation on three key strategic drivers of growth: product innovation, operational excellence, and high-value acquisitions. He applied these strategies across the beverage, restaurant, and snack food categories with dazzling results.

Innovation and high-performance core products brought particular success to beverages and restaurants. In 1986, Calloway's first year at the helm, PepsiCo acquired KFC for $841 million,[20] joining it with Pizza Hut and Taco Bell in PepsiCo's dominant and rapidly expanding restaurant business. With KFC as one of the jewels in what was truly a glittering crown, PepsiCo stepped into leadership positions in all of the fastest-growing quick-service restaurant categories, the category that was already the fastest growing facet of PepsiCo's business. Calloway also led this category to explore home delivery, which at the time was nonexistent, but would go on to become a huge revenue stream.

Steve Reinemund, who served as the CEO of Pizza Hut during this period, described the way that Wayne empowered Pizza Hut's leadership team and encouraged a highly successful expansion into delivery, despite some major problems that bedeviled the restaurant chain at the start:

> Wayne Calloway appointed me the CEO of Pizza Hut in 1986, right after he became PepsiCo's CEO. Previously I had been the head of operations there. At that time, Pizza Hut was the number one pizza restaurant chain in the U.S., but growth was flat. All the growth in the category was going to Domino's, which offered delivery, while we were dine-in and carry out. We had started doing some tests with delivery back when I was the head of operations and we were having pretty poor results.
>
> After I was promoted, we put more pedal to the metal to try to make delivery happen in a way that would work right. But within six months, we were losing a million dollars a

month. That was not good. I went to see Wayne in January 1987 and told him, "Wayne, this plan is not working." His reply was something along the lines of, "Yes, you're right. The plan is not working." At that point, I paused. To be honest, I never understood why, during those six months, Wayne didn't fire me.

But then, I told him, "I have a new plan." I explained it. He told me to make it happen. He said, "You are working in the right area, you've just got to make it work and I believe you can." In the face of the losses we'd had, I couldn't believe he had this confidence. He supported the new plan and stood behind me at a time when most people in his position would have done the exact opposite.

I think that it was within about six months after that meeting, after we had redirected and started following through on our refined plan, that we started to see real results. What that entire experience did for me was literally redefine what was possible and achievable. And it changed the way that all of us on the Pizza Hut leadership team thought about success. It was not marginal and incremental. It was dramatic.

That was what Wayne inspired. He never told me how to do it. He realized the importance of working on the right thing, of having the right people on the project, and then— from his perspective—of supporting it, even during a period of extensive problems. He stuck with us. And, in retrospect, I can say that this experience didn't just produce great results for Pizza Hut. It impacted every single person on this team. Everyone went on to do bigger things, and I believe that everyone performed better and succeeded at a higher level because this experience gave us a very different understanding of what success was and how to achieve it.[21]

During this early period of his leadership of PepsiCo, Calloway's approach also translated into real success in beverages, where PepsiCo's total market share reached a new record, at 31%,[22] after the introduction of Slice into the new juice-added segment of the soft drink market. Meanwhile, sales and operating profits grew dramatically, thanks to a focus on increased operational efficiency.

Early on, we introduced two initiatives that are worth examining within this overall context: "Operation Offset," launched in 1986, and the "Methods Improvement Program," in 1987. Operation Offset promoted the use of technology to cut operational costs, and the "Methods Improvement Program" leveraged Frito-Lay's human capital to cut costs by encouraging employees to submit ideas for improving everyday operations.

Both initiatives fit hand-in-glove with the Calloway Growth Agenda and they delivered valuable results. Let's take a closer look at "Methods Improvement." Who would know more about ways to improve a distribution center's efficiency than the employees who spent their work lives there? In all, thousands of submissions came in each year from employees at every level, and many were tested and implemented across entire business units, saving the company millions of dollars. In the short term alone, this program enabled Frito-Lay to achieve cost savings that minimized losses from a few sub-par product launches in 1987. Although this front-line engagement is more common now, it was very innovative in the 1980s.

"Operation Offset" also benefitted Frito-Lay by introducing handheld computing technology for use by the division's route salesmen. The original objective was to save time, reduce paper-work, and improve order tracking. In what was truly one of the highlights of my career at PepsiCo, I led the team that managed this project.

Wayne played a unique role in the handheld computer (HHC) program. He initially said no to our business case. I went back, did some more work and resubmitted our plan. He said no again. After the third time, I flew up to PepsiCo in Purchase, NY and had a conversation with him in person about the order tracking, time-saving, efficiency, and other potential benefits of the hand-held program. He could tell I was frustrated with him and the process that his most profitable division, Frito-Lay, needed to go through in order to get a $50 million investment in such an obvi-ously valuable initiative.

I recall that meeting so clearly. He sat there calmly and let me talk, expressing my frustrations, and then he quietly told me, "Un-til you show up with a sales leader that has the same passion that you have as the head of technology, I'm going to keep saying no."

His insight was that this effort couldn't be successful if it were viewed by the division as just an IT project. After all, we had thou-sands of salesmen who had been doing the same thing, the same way, for decades. The IT department couldn't change that: only the sales leadership could.

That was a great learning moment for me. On the way back to Dallas, I kept trying to figure out why he hadn't just told me that in the first place. I then realized that he had been trying to figure out *why* I didn't ask him why he kept saying no.

That was the turning point, I reached out to Leo Kiely, who was Frito-Lay's Sales and Marketing Senior Vice President. He understood, agreed and assigned a strong "changeleader"—Ron

Rittenmeyer, Vice President of Sales Operations, to work on building the *real* business case. Ron was tougher on me than Wayne. He kept pushing me to evaluate whether this change was going to increase sales or reduce cost. The question was simple, but the answer was complex. In some districts it would increase sales, in others it would reduce costs, and in many it would do a little bit of both. We got the Line Sales Vice Presidents to engage with their teams. Al Carey was one of those Vice Presidents and is now the Chief Executive Officer of PepsiCo Americas Beverages. He recalled that "the entire sales management team began to understand the potential of the handheld computers to transform the way we went to market and truly professionalized our 10,000 person sales force."

Eventually, the approach that we put together in our final capital request to Wayne and the Board was that we would go district by district, snapshot its selling expense number, and commit to reducing it by 1% of sales by *either* growing sales or reducing cost. Both outcomes were acceptable and in keeping with the Calloway Way of letting us figure it out and then holding us accountable.

The project was ultimately approved, but under rigorous requirements. Not only were these projected outcomes expected to more than pay for the handheld computers, but each District Manager also was required to develop a specific plan for delivering the results. In other words, we respected each unit's autonomy by setting the target, but relying upon the front line to figure out how they were going to get there.

This plan was immediately approved. Soon after that, I saw Wayne in Dallas at an Executive Committee meeting. All he did was wink at me, but I could tell he was very proud of both Ron and me because we had had the courage and commitment to stick to our vision and make it happen. But the people that "owned" it were Al Carey and the other Sales Vice Presidents, the Regional and District Managers and the entire sales force. That was the Calloway Way.

Another example of the Calloway Way was that I had initially asked for $50 million, but what we got approved was $40 million. And we delivered the handheld computers for that lower price tag. Wayne continually told us that too much money makes you sloppy. If he had just signed off on the program initially, the results would not have been nearly as stunning. His simple "no" changed my approach to every success I've had in my career since then.

It's worth taking a moment to examine PepsiCo's 1986 and 1987 acquisitions, as these helped to demonstrate Wayne's vision of PepsiCo's long-term success, which would be achieved through the twin goals of domestic dominance and global expansion. The KFC acquisition not only secured a final leadership position in one of the country's fastest expanding markets but, over time, it went on to pay multinational dividends as well.

In addition, the new CEO achieved an almost immediate payoff from PepsiCo's acquisition of MEI Corporation, Pepsi's third largest bottler, and Seven-Up International, which had a strong global presence. In all, 35% of 1987's earnings per share were attributable to acquisitions carried out under Wayne Calloway's new leadership.[23] And he remained on the hunt for promising targets, soon moving on to acquire snack foods market leaders in Greece, Portugal, and South Korea.

But if acquisitions were a key element in Wayne's quest for bold growth and consistently strong results, so was innovation. In PepsiCo's 1988 Annual Report, he pointed out that heavy snackers accounted for 75% of Frito-Lay sales,[24] while medium-to-light

snackers limited their intake, largely because of health considerations. In response, new light-oil products were introduced. At
the same time, PepsiCo acquired Smartfood, Inc., a healthy snack
producer with an appealing mix of products. But the company
never lost sight of its existing customers: new line extensions
of Fritos, Doritos, and other highly profitable products were introduced during this same period in order to continue to entice
heavy snackers.

With this strong growth agenda front and center, PepsiCo
kept the momentum going by investing heavily in innovation and
business development opportunities across all areas, particularly
restaurants. Pizza Hut's hand-tossed pizzas and new delivery-on-
ly units were revenue boosters. So was Taco Bell's new value-ori-
ented menu, which pumped up sales by broadening the customer
base, especially among families that had previously tended to view
quick-service restaurants as too expensive vis-à-vis value.

At the same time, within beverages and food products, opera-
tions-focused acquisitions were the priority. Following the major
success of the MEI acquisition, which demonstrated the operational efficiencies that could be achieved through consolidation
on this front, PepsiCo spent more than $1.6 billion[25] to acquire
previously independent, small- and medium-sized bottlers.

And the beat went on. A partnership with Hostess Canada improved distribution range and lowered costs, while Plan-o-Gram,
an initiative with roots in the Methods Improvement initiative,
knocked-off 15 to 60 minutes per route salesman in stocking time.
New automatic optical technology was added to Frito-Lay facto-
ries to remove sub-par chips and improve overall quality. Finally,
automated equipment was added to distribution and warehousing
facilities, enabling product to be stocked higher than had been

previously possible. In all, this contributed to a 29% rise in operating profits for food products in 1989.[26]

During that same year, the strategy of "close-in" acquisitions—low-risk, high-yield companies that fit PepsiCo's core competencies—continued, with $4.4 billion spent on purchases[27] aimed at boosting cash flow and raising the corporation's international profile. Two of the U.K.'s leading snack chip producers, 29 bottling companies, and over 700 outstanding franchises were added to the company's assets,[28] with the goals of supporting international growth efforts and capturing profitable domestic opportunities.

And the results were strong. In a strategy reminiscent of his past practice of relying upon Frito-Lay's strong domestic sales to support longer-term-payoff investments in international and innovation, Calloway, as PepsiCo's CEO, used cash flow from savvy domestic acquisitions to help support aggressive bets on future global profits.

The PepsiCo pattern of aggressive acquisitions, with a heavy focus on boosting the corporation's international presence, continued in 1990. Activities included 23 acquisitions, including Mexico's largest cookie company, Gamesa.[29] Additionally, the company maintained its commitment to leveraging new technologies to streamline operations, cut costs, and improve customer service, especially at Frito-Lay. And on other fronts, it was full speed ahead with other expansion efforts, including with restaurant deliveries and enhancements in beverage lines such as Ocean Spray juices and Lipton teas—all aimed at finding new ways to satisfy customer tastes and preferences.

WITH THE RIGHT AGENDA, CHALLENGES ARE MANAGEABLE

Around this time, Frito-Lay and its seemingly unstoppable growth machine encountered some challenges. The way that Wayne and his leadership team responded to these is instructive, especially in the way that the group balanced their shorter- and longer-term management agenda, always with an eye toward growth. This is the way that he described the experience to the Charlotte Chamber of Commerce in a May 1996 speech:

Back in the early '90s, Frito was crunching along at its normal wonderful growth rate. Sales were a little sluggish, but profits were on their historical trend. To the outside world, things looked pretty rosy. But the management at Frito-Lay saw things a little differently. The new president, Roger Enrico, noticed that more and more we had been relying on pricing as a way to grow profits. We were simply raising prices to bring in more money. Which sounds easy—and in fact, it is. But as a long-term strategy, it's about as viable as reducing your package size. You can get away with it for a while, but eventually, consumers begin looking elsewhere, and competitors get big ideas about sliding in under you.

We also noticed that the quality of our products had gone down, almost imperceptibly, each year. But over a decade, the change was significant. For example, to crank up production we had raised the cooking temperature slightly and speeded up the conveyer belt a little. The product was almost as good as it used to be—but not quite. Consumers didn't notice—at least, they didn't know they noticed. But we began losing taste tests against competitors. Worse yet, we started to lose our own age-old challenge: people were able to eat just one. So

Frito-Lay made a big decision. They decided to totally re-engineer their business, to restructure, to reduce headcount, to improve economics.

Now this may sound like a familiar scenario. But there was one very important difference from your average corporate overhaul. At Frito-Lay, they made an unusual commitment to employees: that every penny saved would be put back into quality and ultimately into growth. And to give you some perspective, those pennies added up to about $100 million.

This was not a minor shake-up. The work force shrunk by 1,700 jobs. But the jobs that remained were better jobs with more authority and more opportunity. At the same time, Frito made lots of quality improvements in packaging, in raw materials, even in their advertising and promotions. They started chasing market share once again, really pushing to get every last consumer.

When the smoke cleared two years later, Frito-Lay was growing both sales and earnings at a faster clip than they had in 40 years—nearly 15% a year. And they were doing it by raising per-capita consumption and capturing market share. In other words, not just pricing but real growth.

Out in the marketplace, the impact was enormous. Within a year or so, Borden, their biggest competitor, was almost out of business. Then the English company, United Biscuits, decided to sell Keebler. And last fall, Anheuser-Busch announced it was getting out of the snack business—by selling its Eagle Snacks division.

So, not only was Frito-Lay making big profits, their three biggest national competitors essentially packed it in. Frito-Lay is still growing, adding new sales routes, building plants and capacity, creating new products. They've replaced all those 1,700 jobs and then some, but the jobs were based on real growth. In other words, Frito-Lay is doing everything a re-engineered business is supposed to do—but usually doesn't.

Why did it work? Because the ultimate goal was not just to pull a few more dollars to the bottom line—as attractive as that might be to Chairmen like me. The ultimate goal was to grow the business—and everyone knew it. [And] the people who had to make it all happen saw change as an opportunity not a punishment.

To Calloway, the Frito-Lay restructuring that PepsiCo successfully carried out during this period offered leadership lessons that many different types of organizations could learn from. Here's how he described it during a speech before the Food Marketing Institute in January 1995:

I don't think there's a company on earth that has reorganized, restructured, reconstituted as much as PepsiCo. We seem to re-create ourselves about six times a year as far as I can tell. And while it's saved us plenty of money over the years, it hasn't always made us, at least in my view, a better company. But one of the times it did occurred four years ago, when we restructured our Frito-Lay division. We saved a hundred million dollars. But we also made a commitment—to put every dime of it back into the business. And that's exactly what we did.

Looking back, we missed out on a one-time profit bump any CEO would love. Instead, we invested the money in things that meant something to consumers: better packaging to keep our products fresher and looking better; technology that produced better taste; line extensions that gave people more choices. Things consumers could see, and taste, and touch. As a result, Frito-Lay is scampering around the snack food aisle like a 50-year-old puppy, capturing market share and making more money than anyone ever imagined—for us, and for a lot of you. Frito is growing at 15% a year, which in turn is driving 7% growth in the entire snack-chip category. For retailers, that means higher sales, and higher margins. That's good for us, that's good for you, and that's good for the consumers.

It's worth pointing out that, despite the consistency of Pepsi-Co's exceptional results, the experience of having some ups and downs was virtually inevitable. During 1992, for example, Pepsi-Co took a hit because of a change in an accounting method related to "Employers' Accounting for Postretirement Benefits Other than Pensions," and "Accounting for Income Taxes." These changes alone reduced PepsiCo's operating profit by $73 million.[30]

But regardless of the specific challenges, Calloway's leadership model remained strong. As Roger Enrico, the PepsiCo executive who went on the succeed Wayne Calloway as the corporation's Chairman and CEO, used to say, "Wayne Calloway is a great boss when things are going well, and an even greater boss when they aren't."

THE GLOBALIZATION STRATEGY PAYS OFF

By 1993, PepsiCo's net income and revenue had both strongly rebounded. By this point in PepsiCo's evolution, successful execution of the globalization strategy had really begun to deliver significant rewards. Thanks to extensive restaurant expansion in Europe and Asia, the most highly trafficked Pizza Hut and KFC globally were located in Paris and Hong Kong, respectively.

Some of the most exciting developments during this period took place in beverages. At a CAGNY (Consumer Analyst Group of New York) meeting in Scottsdale, Arizona in February 1995, Calloway spoke about Pepsi-Cola's domestic business and its response to a number of competitive threats:

> Some of you may recall that about two years ago, Craig Weatherup, the Chairman of this business, said to a large group of you that he has three major competitive issues to deal with: Coke, alternative beverages, and private label. Last year, aggressive plans to deal with all three converged on the second quarter. Two were planned. The surprise was private label and the dynamics of the market at that moment.
>
> Private label was on the cusp, gaining share, spreading across the country, but facing the need to lap its aggressive introductions. We had the opportunity to deal it a major blow, because many retailers began looking to pump life into their soft drink business and wanted to work with us. So we offered some terrific deals, huge numbers were accepted, volume exploded, and we had to scramble.
>
> At the same time, to outflank Coke as well as private label, we launched two major initiatives: Freshness Dating for diet products and lots of new packaging. Finally, to expand the successful alternative beverages strategy, we launched a lemonade line and All Sport, our isotonic drink. And we produced an extremely aggressive second-year plan for Lipton. Our iced tea momentum was strong. Coke wasn't particularly focused on teas. And we were the only one with both ends of the market covered well—by that I mean cans and bottles.
>
> So, we made the strategic decision to go for it all and that's

exactly what we did. It made for a painful second quarter, but look at the results! Private label share has declined steadily since April and was down for the year. What was a major threat at this time last year is far less of a threat today. Not out—but certainly down and counting. [Meanwhile] In supermarkets, Brand Pepsi grew 14% for the year—clearly outperforming the competition. [And] Diet Pepsi clearly outperformed the competition, growing almost 8%, with most of the strength coming in the last half of the year after we introduced Freshness Dating.

This period witnessed countless other achievements as well. On the international front, Wayne Calloway's long-standing commitment to global expansion paid off as PepsiCo's penetration of the Mexican snack chip market soared, reaching 80%,[31] which was a higher level even than in the U.S. Meanwhile, some of Pepsi-Co's most vibrant markets grew in Saudi Arabia and Guatemala. Overall brand recognition even increased in Central and Eastern Europe, where, until then, the corporation's market penetration had been low.

All in all, it was a period of great and productive change for the corporation. Over the course of the ten years ending in 1993, Pepsi-Cola's prices declined by 30%, but its profits grew four-fold[32]—a staggering testament to the operational improvements and cost-cutting measures that the CEO and his leadership team had consistently remained focused upon.

Meanwhile, the restaurant business thrived as well. Calloway described that growth journey during his CAGNY 1995 speech:

At PepsiCo, our restaurant revenue went from zero in 1977 to more than nine billion dollars by 1993. Our operating profit went from zero to almost $780 million by 1993, a compound growth rate of more than 17%. How many businesses in the world have grown profits at 17% a year for about 15 years?

Our position in the industry also increased...We went from 11% of a $67 billion industry [in 1988] to more than 14% of an $85 billion industry in 1993, and became an acknowledged industry leader. This is really top performance based on any measure.

A CONSISTENT LEADERSHIP AGENDA DRIVES CONSISTENT RESULTS

Throughout his leadership career, first at Frito-Lay and then as the CEO of PepsiCo, Wayne Calloway never lost his commitment to the growth agenda and his razor-sharp focus on delivering strong and consistent results. 1995 was his final year as Chairman and CEO. By then, PepsiCo had grown to become the third-largest corporation in the world,[33] while achieving its long-heralded vision of becoming a top-tier player in restaurant, beverage, and snack food markets around the globe with highly successful expansions into China, Saudi Arabia, the U.K., and South Africa.

An in-depth look at PepsiCo's breadth and depth in 1995 is revealing, since this is the corporation that he and his growth-oriented agenda built. With approximately 480,000 employees, more than 120,000 men and women were based outside the U.S.[34] The roster of best-selling brands was truly awe-inspiring. Overall sales topped $30 billion, including $10.4 billion in beverages, $8.5 billion in snack foods, and $11.3 billion in restaurants. All in all, nearly $8 billion worth of revenues came from international markets across all three segments.[35]

Roger Enrico, who stepped into the role of PepsiCo's Chairman and CEO in 1996, announced Wayne Calloway's retirement with moving words in the corporation's annual report:

> After ten years as Chairman and Chief Executive Officer of PepsiCo, my great friend Wayne Calloway stepped down as CEO in April 1996 and as chairman in November.
>
> Wayne, who remains on the Board of Directors, leaves behind a remarkable legacy of leadership and growth. During his tenure at the top, PepsiCo's sales more than tripled, and the market value of PepsiCo grew by more than $35 billion.
>
> The Calloway era can also be defined in very human terms. His warmth, optimism, integrity, and unwavering belief in the ability of people to grow have left an indelible mark on PepsiCo. More than a gifted leader, he's also a powerful inspiration to all of us who work at PepsiCo.[36]

How did Wayne Calloway and the truly extraordinary corporation he led accomplish all that they did? It's worth concluding this chapter's discussion of "Delivering with Consistency" by looking back at a speech he gave at Sacred Heart University in June 1994:

> Every year, we grow by the equivalent of a Seagram or Upjohn or Hershey Foods. The fact is, this relentless drive for growth has dramatic implications for our performance.
>
> First, we set very ambitious goals for our managers, goals that drive us to be much more ambitious in the marketplace than a company content with modest or slow growth—to constantly come up with bigger, more creative ideas that will make consumers sit up and take notice. And each year, as our chal-

lenge grows, we have to respond in bigger and better ways.

Take new products, for example. In 1990, our four most successful new products generated nearly $500 million in retail sales. That was pretty good. Most big companies, even today, would be ecstatic. But just a few years later, in 1993, our four biggest new products produced retail sales in excess of a billion dollars. I'm talking about our Lipton Original Tea, Big Foot Pizza, Colonel's Rotisserie Gold Chicken, and Doritos Tortilla Thins.

So, you begin to see that to achieve really big growth requires an extraordinarily aggressive approach, stretch goals, thinking in much grander terms than ordinary companies, working relentlessly to improve upon a performance that would leave other businesses feeling pretty content. And integral to that is a management style that gives people the freedom to act boldly, to really achieve their potential.

To Wayne Calloway, it was always all about people. As Indra Nooyi, PepsiCo's Chairman and CEO, recalled:

> Wayne constantly stressed the need for talent. He believed that talent trumped everything else. He was convinced that, if you recruited and developed great talent, then all the business problems could be handled and those great people would achieve the growth and other results that PepsiCo was focused on.[37]

In the next chapter, I will discuss the third essential element in Wayne Calloway's leadership model: "Building a Great Team." Achieving this depended upon creating and sustaining an empowering organizational culture, one that was built upon a foundation of integrity and a commitment.

NOTES

1. Andrea Rothman, "Can Wayne Calloway Handle The Pepsi Challenge?" *BusinessWeek*, January 26, 1992.

2. Ibid.

3. Constance L. Hays, "Wayne Calloway Dies at 62; Was Chief at PepsiCo 10 Years," *The New York Times*, July 10, 1998.

4. PepsiCo, Inc., Annual Report, 1996.

5. Ibid.

6. Ibid.

7. Ibid.

8. U.S. Securities and Exchange Commission, "1995 Annual Report: PepsiCo, Inc.," http://www.getfilings.com/o0000077476-96-000023.html.

9. Ibid.

10. PepsiCo, Inc, "1996 Selected Financial Data," http://www.pepsico.com/Annual-Reports/1996/selecteddata.html.

11. See note 8 above.

12. Joe McCann, Interview, 2014.

13. PepsiCo, Inc., Annual Report, 1978.

14. PepsiCo, Inc., Annual Report, 1979.

15. PepsiCo, Inc., Annual Report, 1980.

16. PepsiCo, Inc. Annual Report, 1981.

17. PepsiCo, Inc. Annual Report, 1983.

18. Joe McCann, Interview, 2014.

19. Peggy Moore, Interview, 2014.

20. PepsiCo, Inc., Annual Report, 1986.

21. Steve Reinemund, Interview, 2014.

22. See note 20 above.

23. PepsiCo, Inc., Annual Report, 1987.

24. Ibid.

25. PepsiCo, Inc., Annual Report, 1988.

26. PepsiCo, Inc., Annual Report, 1989.

27. Ibid.

28. Ibid.

29. PepsiCo, Inc., Annual Report, 1990.

30. See note 8 above.

31. PepsiCo, Inc. "The PepsiCo Family." http://www.pepsico.eu/company/the-pepsico-familya-americas-foods.html.

32. PepsiCo, Inc., Annual Report, 1993.

33. PepsiCo, Inc., Annual Report, 1995.

34. PepsiCo, Inc., Annual Report, 1996, online version.

35. Ibid.

36. PepsiCo, Inc., Annual Report, 1996.

37. Indra K. Nooyi, Interview, 2014.

CHAPTER FOUR

BUILDING A GREAT TEAM

THE LEADERSHIP JOURNEY

The remainder of this book is about the "mojo" of how PepsiCo was able to achieve these aggressive growth agendas, with decades of consistently impressive results, by building a great team.

As PepsiCo grew, the team also grew to over 400,000 people.[1] Our principles for leadership development and our approach to expanding our human capital were key to achieving our results. And I believe that they are durable and applicable today to every enterprise. They are absolutely key to playing and winning in the competitive world we live in.

As I emphasized in my earlier book, *Blind Spot*,[2] of all the levers that matter, successful alignment between an enterprise's Business Model and its Organizational Model "matters the most." Many companies possess or can obtain the financial capital required to grow. However, they often underinvest in the human capital that is needed to drive sustainable results. The key components of this Organizational Model are: Structure, Talent, Culture, and Leadership.

Wayne Calloway was the master integrator and harmonizer of these components. He wove these four elements into the fabric of PepsiCo for almost a quarter of a century. He recognized that his major role was not to be the dominant product, sales, financial, manufacturing or marketing leader. Instead, he believed his major role and responsibility was to build a great team of people that were "the best of the best" in each discipline so they could then do the best job of growing revenue, building brands, managing cost and quality, and so forth.

While serving as Executive in Residence at Wichita State University in 1987, he delivered a speech that focused largely on the essential importance of human capital, emphasizing, "The secret to our success—secret to any successful organization—you can say it in one word, and that's 'people'... Corporations don't do anything—it's all people."

Indeed, it was part of the brilliance of his leadership model that his approach—which proved its value countless times and in countless ways throughout this era—was based upon fundamental assumptions about finding, inspiring, and trusting the right people, who would then work together to achieve shared objectives.

In an article that appeared about Wayne Calloway after his death in July 1998, the *New York Times* highlighted his truly exceptional focus and expertise when it came to talent:

> "The thing I always admired about him was his insight into people," said John F. Welch Jr., the chairman of G.E., who called Mr. Calloway, who joined the G.E. board in 1991, "a beautiful man" who displayed great courage during his long illness. "He could really read people. People we had known

the way of people who work for you. Let them do their thing. Guide them. Cheerlead. Remove obstacles. But let *them* get it done. I know it's easy to say. And I know it's tough to do. But there's only one way you're going to free yourself of that burden: Hire good people, and get out of the way.

This chapter will describe the elements of building a great team and explore the way that each element influences, and integrates with, the others.

DESIGNING THE RIGHT STRUCTURE

The way an enterprise is structured establishes how an organization thinks about accountability and decision-making, and it reflects the primary "power alleys" of the business model.

For example, Walmart was structured with a very dominant center, reflecting a business model that was built around leveraging supply chain power. Since all suppliers were directed to Bentonville, Arkansas and away from selling to each store, Walmart was able to amass significant purchasing leverage, thereby changing the competitive landscape in retail. The stores were an extension of the "core" and were highly standardized from city to city.

Home Depot started with a very different business model. The dominant notion behind its franchise was the local hardware store. Home Depot recognized that not just every city, but every neighborhood, had a personality. Products, price, and staffing were strongly focused on local constituencies, preferences, and cultures. Home Depot's power alley was based upon knowing its customer, and its model was highly store-manager centric. The company knowingly left significant purchasing power on the cutting floor because their Atlanta center was not operationally intrusive.

It's clear that while both of these models were successful, each has its own set of strengths and weaknesses. These two examples (one of high centralization, the other of significant decentralization) have since begun to give way to a different framework, driven by the business necessity of being both highly leveraged along the dimensions of cost and quantity *and* also creating a unique and personalized experience for each customer at the point of sale.

The modern business model has become an "and/and" instead of an "either/or": a model that has been driven by the influence of Amazon's successful model, which pairs a highly leveraged, common back end with a customer-unique front end. This customer-centric model, when combined with powerful supply chain economics, has dramatically changed the retail landscape yet again.

There are some key thoughts that should be reinforced by these examples. First, structure matters (which was a core premise that Wayne Calloway understood and appreciated); and second, the Industrial Era structures of either centralization or decentralization have given way to a more complex hybrid. The focus of these hybrids has changed the dialogue from an all-in centralized or decentralized structure to a more granular design that distinguishes between which capabilities and structures should be "common" and which should remain "unique."

Globalization and modern technologies have accelerated this dialogue. Companies that historically have been decentralized are having trouble gaining cost leverage or consistent quality, and they are not consistently able to serve customers that span geographies, channels or product lines. Those that have been very centralized are struggling to serve the unique needs of customers in, for example, Europe vs. Africa vs. Asia. Before any enterprise swings too far in either direction, it needs to really be thoughtful about this, making certain not to solve one set of problems by creating another. Executive teams need to take the time to think through the best way to design a hybrid structure.

It was this type of approach to structure design that made PepsiCo so successful for decades. Don Kendall, Herman Lay, Andy Pearson, and Wayne Calloway each understood that because their divisions and geographies were unique in so many ways, especially within a company with hundreds of thousands of people at the point of transaction, the power to make decisions to reflect these differences had to be distributed. There were, however, certain things within the company that needed to be common.

This is the current dialogue in many companies. Yet this thoughtful dialogue at PepsiCo, and the resulting approach to organizational management, was way ahead of its time.

The PepsiCo Business Model was created jointly by its entrepreneurial cofounders, Herman Lay and Don Kendall. It was then commercialized by Andy Pearson, PepsiCo's first President, and finally institutionalized and globally scaled by Wayne, as the corporation grew to be one of the largest and most-respected companies in the world.

To provide some overall context, PepsiCo was originally established in the mid-1960s as a pure holding company. PepsiCo's corporate headquarters (then in New York City) was to be small and noninvasive, with the Division Presidents held fully accountable for success. In conjunction with this structure, it's worth noting that success was clearly to be defined at the corporate level. Key success measures included growth of revenue, market share, new products, channels, P&L, capital expenditures, return on assets, SG&A targets, and so forth. Within this structure, each division was then empowered to figure out how to achieve target results—and make that happen.

The result was empowerment, but this existed within a system that set boundaries and targets that were focused on tough results. Senior executives, managers, and teams could take many paths to get to the goals. However, there were also clear rules as to how to play the game that insisted on integrity, or "doing the right things the right way." That framework gave all of us the cohesiveness and the "borders" of the game.

There's a story that Wayne Calloway used to like to tell—in fact, he told it in a number of speeches and meetings. It clearly embodied, for him, a vision of how the corporation's decentralized structure and focus on personal empowerment (along with an equally strong focus on personal responsibility) combined to enable PepsiCo to achieve its growth agenda while also doing business the right way. This dramatic version of the story comes from a June 1994 speech that he delivered at Sacred Heart University:

> Let me share an example of…a guy named Alexander Antoniadi. Alexander's not a big executive at PepsiCo, but he's a terrific example of the kind of people we need [in order] to succeed.
>
> You see, a few years ago, Alexander was running our Pizza Hut right in the middle of Moscow. Good job, interesting timing. Because, as you might remember, three years ago, one hot Sunday night in the summer, the infamous Russian coup began. President Gorbachev was locked in a country house. Tanks were rolling through the streets of Moscow, and there

were new people in charge at the Kremlin. Imagine the moment. A government is overthrown, a new one is in place. They control the army, the radio stations, just about everything.

And just as the coup is hitting its stride, one force stands up to it and says: "No. We won't go along!" If you remember, it was the Russian Parliament, led by Boris Yeltsin. Early Monday morning, they announce their opposition to the coup and lock themselves in the Parliament Building. CNN has cameras all over the place. President Bush rushes back to Washington. The world is at the brink. As the hours pass and the tension mounts, guess what happens. The Russian Parliament begins to get hungry. But there's no food. More hours pass. The tension continues to build.

Finally, they can stand it no more. What do they do? Well, they did what any of us would do in the same situation—they sent out for pizza. This really happened. One of Boris Yeltsin's aides gets on the phone to our Moscow Pizza Hut and orders 300 large pies to go.

Now, the Pizza Hut manager, our Russian friend Alexander, is faced with a very big decision. At this point, nobody knows who's going to eventually win. Will the coup succeed? At this point, it certainly looks like it will.

If Pizza Hut fills the order and offends the Soviet conspirators, his Pizza Hut is probably closed forever, along with our 34 Pepsi plants throughout the nation. Alexander probably ends up in Siberia.

But Alexander doesn't hesitate a minute. He throws the kitchen into overdrive and, in an hour or so, delivers 300 pepperoni pizzas to the Russian Parliament, dodging tanks and artillery placements along the way. And risking our entire

Pizza Hut and Pepsi-Cola business.

Alexander doesn't call his regional manager in London. He doesn't call headquarters in New York. He's decided that, Siberia or no Siberia, he's going to fill the order.

A day later, the coup fails. Thank God. And the whole world, including President Bush, is trying to reach Boris Yeltsin and his associates on the phone. But the leaders of the Russian Parliament, the heroes of the day, aren't taking calls. They're not making them either. Except one. At midday, in Alexander's Pizza Hut, the phone rings once more. He picks it up and there's a top Parliament official on the phone, thanking him for the pizzas. "We loved your pizza. We won't forget," he said. And I don't think they will.

Now, Alexander Antoniadi may not yet be a business legend, but he's the embodiment of what we're all about. He's bright. He thinks quickly in a tough situation. He's highly autonomous. And he operates one of our thousands of small, local units.

Most of our managers don't get a chance to become part of a Russian Revolution. But all of them are empowered to grow their business, whether it's a restaurant, a sales route, or an entire division.

Within PepsiCo's system, it was up to each division how it organized itself, sequenced investment, and took risks on products, pricing, and promotions. So one might best describe this as "directed decentralization" or a "Federalist" model.

Within this "Federalist" model, the Operating Divisions understood how to operate independently, because each division had been established according to a different business model. For example, Frito-Lay was initially made up of 32 regions. It competed at those regional levels, with no national leverage or synergy coming from corporate headquarters. At that time Frito-Lay's competitors and customers were all regional. In fact, prior to the interstate highway system and the mainframe computer, business models were mostly local or regional.

During the late 1960s and into the 1970s, Frito-Lay changed its business model to reflect the changing needs of our customers, driven by the demands of Walmart, the first major national retailer. We began a transformation and became a national powerhouse with a leveraged, functional business model. Purchasing, Manufacturing, Distribution, Sales, Finance, Marketing, and Human Resources became large national organizations, focused on functional excellence. In addition, we built a centralized system group that enabled the functions to standardize and work together. As CEO of Frito-Lay, Calloway drove most of that change (as we discussed in detail in Chapter 2, "Setting the Agenda"). As described in Chapter 3, "Delivering with Consistency," Frito-Lay grew at roughly 15% revenue and profit growth, compounded for almost 20 years. That was the right business model for Frito-Lay.

Our sister division, Pepsi-Cola, however, had a different business model because its decentralization was based upon a structural franchise system. Each geography was an independent bottler that was fighting it out with Coca-Cola, Dr. Pepper, and other regional franchisees. These bottlers were also expected to meet the objectives that PepsiCo corporate set out for them, but they were able to take their own, different pathway. Other divisions at the time, like Wilson Sporting Goods and North American Van Lines, took a different approach. Meanwhile, since PepsiCo also had some international snack food and beverage divisions, each country was enabled to set its own approach to its business model and, therefore, its own level of centralization and decentralization.

Within PepsiCo's largely decentralized structure, there were a couple of functions that had a global corporate overlay. Those were, in fact, what made this complex system work. First, Finance had a strong tie from each division to Corporate. This ensured the necessary controls and ethical structures that were required in a public company. There were very few surprises or scandals. You couldn't hide problems, at least not for very long. The Corporate Finance operation allocated capital to the divisions. Of course, this was a fairly standard approach for holding companies and multinationals during that era. Effectively, it was Finance that was "Headquarters" to most business units or divisions for conglomerates of that era.

What was unique at PepsiCo, by design, was that a similar model existed for Human Resources. It was structured like Finance with "hard tethers" into the divisions and geographies. The HR function was comparable in power and prestige to Finance and, just like Finance, which maintained the integrity of financial systems, HR maintained "people-systems" consistency. This was by design so that the quality and quantity of leadership talent was never an impediment to growth or performance.

It's useful to look back on the way that Wayne Calloway described the big picture rationale behind PepsiCo's decentralized structure. During his June 1994 speech at Sacred Heart University, he explained:

> When you get right down to it, how you manage a business is shaped by your customers, your markets, and your resources. But it also has an awful lot to do with something much more

abstract—human potential. Or, more specifically, managing your people to bring all their creativity, skills, and ability to bear on your business.

Now, bringing out the best in people is important for any company. But for PepsiCo, it's absolutely crucial. Let me tell you why. There are really two reasons. The first has to do with growth. The second concerns the nature of our products and distribution system…

You see, what we sell are little luxuries. Don't think of us as a traditional packaged goods company, as good as they are. Don't think of us like a seller of soap or tissues or even breakfast cereal, all of which people need. Because most of our products retail for less than a dollar or two, and, let's face it, even at that price, nobody really needs them.

On top of that, we sell them in literally hundreds of thousands of small outlets, spread across nearly 170 countries. Our restaurant system alone includes over 24,000 individual Pizza Hut, KFC, and Taco Bell units, serving some 10 million customers a day.

Our soft drinks and snacks are delivered by over 20,000 of our own route salesmen who, like our restaurants, operate a lot like small, independent businesses…

Just for contrast, think about Boeing, a great company, but you probably couldn't find a business more different than PepsiCo. With manufacturing highly concentrated, a key customer list you could probably fit on one page, and products that cost millions of times what you'd pay for a Pepsi or a taco, the dynamics of Boeing are the polar opposite of ours…For Boeing, a centralized, hierarchical structure would seem to make sense. In fact it's probably essential…

[But] our business doesn't rise and fall on the skills of a few top salespeople. Our success rests in the hands of thousands of local managers. And to be effective they need a tremendous degree of autonomy. That's why PepsiCo is, and always has been, a highly decentralized organization. That's why our management style is so profoundly focused on encouraging individual initiative, and providing an environment in which people at all levels can achieve their full potential.

It may be counterintuitive, but our powerful Human Resources function was put in place to enable this degree of decentralization, but only through a global consistency of leadership philosophy, talent, and values, which was necessary to empower so many people at the point of transaction. As a leader you were considered a PepsiCo executive "on loan" to a business unit in order to enable that structure, and, just as Wayne himself moved from Frito-Lay to PepsiCo headquarters, it was common to move between units and divisions. Meanwhile, performance standards were well known and extremely high. Calloway, Pearson, and the divisional and unit CEOs all travelled with their CFOs and HR leaders. The Finance and HR functions made us a growth company without limits, as they created strong functional leaders and general managers.

I will spend more time on this in sections that follow on Talent, Culture, and Leadership. But before concluding this discussion, it's important to emphasize that each of these key elements were powerfully enabled by PepsiCo's unusual but well-designed structure. Over the years, there were many cases made for centralizing IT or Supply Chain or Distribution. These arguments all made sense from a synergy, leverage, and cost perspective, but they came in conflict with the overall business model and, although tempting financially, they were rejected philosophically. Only HR and Finance were the core PepsiCo structure, and that was by design.

TALENT MATTERS

The renowned and often imitated PepsiCo Human Resources system was just that: a systematic approach to recruiting, developing, assessing, and managing talent at every level of the enterprise. Every company does some or all of these things, but in most cases HR leadership is a secondary support function. At PepsiCo, this was *the* priority, because PepsiCo's leaders believed deeply that growth would not be limited by capital investments or opportunities—but instead, it could only be limited by the lack of necessary human capital to lead and manage at every level across the globe.

This focus on talent was architected by Andy Pearson, during his years as PepsiCo's first president, and Don Kendall, cofounder and then-CEO. However, it was fully embraced, nurtured, and firmly institutionalized during the Calloway era. Wayne made it a way of life and a major component of each leader's performance and compensation.

All too many corporate leaders pay lip service to the importance of human capital but then spend as little time as possible thinking about HR-related matters. But Calloway gave HR the time and resources necessary to succeed because he recognized the essential way that the corporation's meteoric growth depended upon its people, and therefore, its people systems.

His comments at a PepsiCo Personnel Conference in April 1994 offer a useful insight into his perspective on the Human

Resources function:

> HR plays a big role in the success of PepsiCo. The fact is, ours
> is a people business and you're the gatekeepers of talent, the
> first step in the screening process. You're also the standard
> bearers—you help establish and communicate the culture, val-
> ues, and vision of the company. Those are big responsibilities.

During speeches and meetings, he often returned to these
themes: the essential importance of human capital to PepsiCo's
successful growth, and the related essential importance of the HR
function. In a speech before the "Executive Leadership Council"
in Washington, DC in October 1994, he stated simply: "It's no
secret that we hire the best people—and then challenge them to
become ever better. And it's a good thing, too. Because our businesses are about as competitive as any you'll find."

Here's how he described the HR mandate during a speech at a
PepsiCo Personnel Conference in April 1994:

> At PepsiCo, we have a goal. It's not modest, but it is simple.
> We want to be the world's best consumer products compa-
> ny. When you're in people-intensive businesses like ours that
> means we need to recruit and hire and develop the best people
> on earth. In fact, hundreds of thousands of them…
>
> I'm certain we'll never achieve our goal, we'll never at-
> tract and retain and develop the world's best people, *unless*
> we can become the most open and most welcoming, most
> caring company in the world. A company free of artificial
> obstacles, where people are judged not on who they know or
> where they're from, or what they look like, but on what they
> accomplish. A company where individuals can preserve their

distinctive qualities so long as they share high integrity and a deep commitment to results.

Calloway genuinely believed what most people just say: that the greatest asset any organization has is the talent, commitment, and energy of the people who work to produce its products or services each day. How that talent, commitment, and energy is directed and developed is a key indicator of long-term success.

Managing the performance of an organization requires discipline and accountability. The PepsiCo Talent Management System presented throughout these pages encompassed a systematic approach to performance, development, and succession planning, as well as methods for evaluating and rewarding performance outcomes.

The art of engaging people to perform to their optimum ability is much more difficult to describe. It entails creating an organizational climate where people thrive and their passion for the work at hand is ignited. Central to this idea is an understanding of what nurtures, motivates, and rewards the human spirit.

Wayne understood that underlying all human activity is a drive for meaning. People spend one half of their waking life and much of their personal energy at work. It is critical that each individual believes that the path he or she is on is worth the effort and is important to the fulfillment of a larger goal. For human passion to be ignited and harnessed at work, people must find a meaningful purpose in what they do. "Meaningful purpose" is evidenced by each member of the team having a sense of connection and commitment.

Wayne thought and talked about this a great deal throughout his career. In an Executive in Residence speech at Wichita State

University back in 1987, he emphasized, "Business is a lot more than just selling products and making money. It's leadership. It's initiative. It's teamwork, energy, pride, satisfaction. Most of all, it's integrity."

Years later, in a 1994 speech at Sacred Heart University, he commented:

> At PepsiCo, in our free-flowing, fast-moving atmosphere, things move fast. And you just don't have time to worry about being blind-sided or about people shading the truth to cover up their lack of knowledge.
>
> The best businesses have a free and open environment in which people level with one another and are willing to discuss any business issue without recrimination. That's important, because I believe there's no business problem that can't be solved, if it gets the attention of the right people…It has everything to do with character, with human interaction, with our ability to deal with others, honestly and effectively.
>
> And when you think about it, that's not surprising. You see, businesses—big business, small business, corporations, agencies, banks, investment firms—they're all very human places. Business is not theoretical, although theory is important. But ideas by themselves won't get the ball across the goal line. They won't set the cash register ringing.
>
> Business is very emotional and very physical. It's buying and selling and showing up every day. It's dealing with people's livelihoods. And that means dealing with their lives. It requires sensitivity and stamina and a lot of courage and character.

Wayne made sure that each of his leaders understood the vital importance of helping their teams connect with the larger purpose and values that gave meaning to their work. By providing people at all levels with everyday opportunities to contribute, PepsiCo leaders were therefore able to empower these teams to connect with the corporation's core objectives and agenda.

This belief that *talent matters* and that every individual has great potential, was truly the philosophical underpinning of the PepsiCo HR model. This model consisted of several components: Performance Management, Career Development, Talent Management, Succession Planning, Recruiting, and Training. Most companies have the majority of these processes—but this is much more the case today than it was twenty and thirty years ago, when PepsiCo was truly in the vanguard in terms of its strategic management of human capital.

During this era at PepsiCo, we had integrated every one of these key components into our HR system. But there was another crucial element that made this engine hum, which was that this was all considered to be the work of each leader and not simply the HR team.

The way we managed performance set the bar for the other components of the system. To take a more in-depth look at this system, let me focus on a number of significant aspects:

Line organizations owned the performance management process.

At PepsiCo, business unit management was ultimately responsible for the overall performance of an organization. As such, line organizations were the primary owners of the performance management system. Staff organizations, such as Human Resources, served as a partner to enable line management to develop, implement, and continuously improve performance.

Both managers and employees played a critical role in improving organizational performance.

Leadership and employees were expected to work together to consistently improve individual and organizational performance. While leadership needed to be able to effectively manage the skills and ignite the passions and energy of people in a way that openly valued and rewarded their contribution, each individual was accountable for his or her own performance and contribution.

Performance was measured on two dimensions: performance of objectives and demonstration of competencies and values.

Performance was not only determined by *what* we accomplished but also by *how* we accomplished it. Measuring business results against written performance objectives spoke to what we had accomplished. Competency mastery—the ability to demonstrate the thinking, planning, and relationship skills that allowed us to work together in an efficient, effective, and productive manner—provided a second, but equally important, measure of performance (in other words, what also mattered was, "how we got there"). Demonstration of the values of the organization was an essential part of what it meant to be "competent."

Performance had to be differentiated.

In order for the performance bar to be raised across an organization in a meaningful way, exceptional performance needed to be recognized and rewarded differently than solid performance, and solid performance differently than poor performance. In addition to each manager being able to differentiate among members of his or her own work group, it was critical that performance be calibrated across work groups. This assured that expectations and accomplishments for similar jobs were viewed consistently across the organization, and that several members of management had the opportunity to provide feedback for each individual under review.

Performance contributions were tied directly to compensation. In a pay-for-performance system, performance levels were rewarded differently. Compensation in the form of incentive pay and merit increases varied depending on overall contribution levels.

Performance improvement required feedback, coaching, and developmental opportunities.
A primary responsibility of leadership was to coach the development of others. In addition to formal performance management activities, great leaders continuously expected to use *teachable moments*, naturally occurring opportunities to provide performance feedback and coaching. Coaching improvement or reinforcing desired performance close to the time of the event ensured learning and supported trust.

The continuous nature of this Management System allowed PepsiCo to have good working relationships between managers and employees and eliminated the element of surprise at the time of the performance evaluation meeting.

These processes, when done properly, are extremely time consuming and therefore must be a priority that is re-enforced by the leadership team. Under Wayne's leadership, there was a top-down

HR calendar with a cadence much like what we had around business and financial performance. Each quarter, we were either reviewing performance, succession planning or career development moves, promotions, or compensation.

Contrast this with the norm at many other organizations. Either senior managers don't spend enough high-quality time on talent management because they are "busy," or the organization is "siloed" and doesn't encourage constructive collaboration or sharing resources. Or managers may be unwilling to differentiate their people as top, average, and underperformers because it is easier not to make the calls. Finally, it's all too often the case that managers want to hoard top talent so that *they* can be successful.

All of these obstacles were removed at PepsiCo where they would have been considered career-limiting behaviors. The talent reviews that I attended with Calloway, Pearson, Roger Enrico, Mike Jordan, and the key HR leaders were as intense and as grueling as financial, project, product, and marketing reviews. The active preparation for these review sessions each quarter were part of the "Rhythm of Life" for PepsiCo executives and were seen as being open, candid discussions where both assessment of talent and development were key objectives.

One might wonder if this came across as a time-waster. But, in fact, it was difficult to complain about the time investment when the company's Chairman and Division Presidents spent so much of their year focusing on questions like:

- If you were to leave or get promoted who are your replacements?

- What is your plan to deal with bottom-group performance issues?

- Why didn't you do what you told us you would do about your bottom performers last quarter?

- When can we promote or reassign people in your top group?

- What is your plan to backfill people in your top group if we reassign them?

- How far can this person go? What is his/her upside potential?

- What is your recruiting strategy? Which universities are you cultivating?

The questions were exhaustive, as we would talk about two levels of direct reports, one at a time, several times a year. The way an executive embraced these issues had a *significant* impact on his or her own performance, compensation, and promotion potential. So, this really, really mattered to you. Wayne and his leadership team made it personal.

There were a number of the senior leader reviews that Wayne personally conducted. He focused on the top 500 leaders.

However, Vice Presidents, Directors, and Managers were also required to conduct similar sessions with their groups. The Human Resources team brought the standards, tools, and leadership to ensure consistency to each group at every level, and they had the skills, power, and financial support from Calloway, who made it his priority. Unlike most HR functions in other businesses, HR always had a seat at the Chairman's or Division President's table.

Again, this was not considered a luxury, but rather, a necessity. There were a significant number of management development PhDs in each unit because of the direct tie between our growth agenda and our business model, which required a large number of P&L and functional leaders. The genius of that fabulous growth era was the connection between our strategy, the number of P&L managers that the model created, and the number of people required with the skills to lead and manage a complex, global business whose plan it was to double every five years. During the last five years of Wayne's leadership, PepsiCo was adding tens of thousands of people to the company every year. Growth, acquisitions, high performance standards, and a commitment to promote from within meant that PepsiCo's talent system needed to produce 200 executives every year.

To that end, movement of high-potential leaders was swift. It was more the norm than the exception to find 30-year-old VPs and 35-year-old Sr. VPs or Division Presidents. The approach and pathways to these incredible management opportunities were exciting for smart, ambitious leaders (while also being very threatening to bureaucratic, risk-averse managers).

It's interesting to consider the ways that Wayne described the kind of people who would be right for PepsiCo, as well as the type of corporate environment in which they would thrive and be likeliest to be successful. Here's what he had to say at the Mars/Hostess/Frito-Lay Luncheon in July 1994:

> [The] fact is, we seek growth not just to satisfy PepsiCo shareholders, but to meet your personal needs. Growth is necessary to satisfy all of *you*. You're the ones who make the biggest demands, push the hardest, and drive the fastest. You push yourselves harder than anybody would ever think possible— because you need it.
>
> The fact is, most of you signed on with PepsiCo because it's a growth company, and the minute it stopped, you'd disappear faster than a bag of Lay's at a World Cup party. Growth

is what builds teamwork. It's what drives creativity. It's what satisfies your career ambitions and your personal needs…

You see, the fun is in the stretch. You—all our employees—are very ambitious, aggressive people. Strong growth allows us to fulfill our personal needs.

Recruiting and retaining the right talent were among Wayne's highest priorities. In order to achieve this, several integrated streams needed to come together.

First and foremost, our recruiting approach was second to none. We recruited at the best schools, and Wayne himself, as well as the Division Leader and HR, were all involved in the recruiting process. PepsiCo would focus on not just grades and degrees but on all aspects of the individual. We had a shared idea of what kind of intellect and spirit we were looking for in our recruits. We all instinctively could envision if that person could be successful at PepsiCo.

This system required that the most successful Line Leaders, as well as the Chairman himself, needed to spend a lot of time on recruiting, interviewing, and selecting. This was not considered something that could be delegated during the Calloway era, and Wayne was the role model for personal involvement.

During her interview for this book, Indra Nooyi, PepsiCo's Chairman and CEO, recalled her own meeting with Wayne Calloway when she was first interviewing for a job at the corporation:

I remember that I spoke for about fifty-seven minutes and Wayne spoke for three. But he probed at the right times to get me to say what I really felt and to determine my values and how I operated. As I grew to realize later on, he expected everyone to have a point of view, and he wanted to know what that was.[6]

At a Personnel Meeting in May 1995, Wayne offered this advice to the HR team regarding who to look for when building PepsiCo's talent team, and how to find the "right" people:

Keep an open mind. Use all our research, our data, our experience, everything we've learned about people since Pepsi-Co was created. But don't let it limit you. Look in places we've never looked before. Maybe for people we've never considered before. Be as creative as any advertising director. As resourceful and innovative as any product development manager. Use what we've learned as a guideline, and be rigorous in upholding quality standards.

But remember that there are lots of people out there with the power to move our business but who may be cut from a different cloth. You must constantly think in new ways about your goal and how to accomplish it. Keep an open mind and I believe you'll find enough great people to ensure that PepsiCo is a strong and successful company for as far out as we can see.

Once selected to join PepsiCo, an individual would be assigned to a division and a position. The subtle but critical difference between PepsiCo and other corporations was that the assignment would be considered temporary. You weren't, in most cases, hired into a job. Like the military, you were only "on loan" to that unit for a period of time. If you were a high potential leader, you were considered to be "Calloway's" property. That was an extraordinary opportunity—and experience—for anyone fortunate enough to fall into this category. Similarly, PepsiCo HR executives were always on the lookout for talent, even if they didn't have an open position. Although headcount was carefully managed, outstanding talent wasn't turned away because we didn't have a job for them at that moment. And that didn't just apply to executives at the top. Division Presidents would often hire a larger crop of college graduates, or top talent at any level, knowing that we would need them down the line. Some divisions had accelerated development programs where individuals were over-hired for positions and then given ad hoc projects to get them ready to fill in gaps in the talent pipeline.

Wayne's own perspective on his role may have been unique in the corporate world. In an article that appeared in *Beverage Digest* in July 1998, after he had passed away, Phil Dusenberry, Chairman of BBDO NY, recalled that Wayne used to say that his job at Pepsi was "to keep the eagles flying in formation." Mr. Dusenberry noted: "He spotted talent, found good people and let them flourish. He empowered them to be their best."[7]

Indeed, looking back on that era, it is remarkable how many extremely strong leaders PepsiCo developed during these years— and how well Wayne kept them "flying in formation," despite the challenges embodied by that simple concept.

Along those same lines, Peggy Moore, who worked with Wayne for many years, in roles that included Vice President of Human Resources and Vice President of Investor Relations, shared these insights:

> Wayne was particularly gifted at getting the eagles to fly in formation—there were a lot of strong, talented, people at PepsiCo, and he could really get them all to work together very effectively.

It's somewhat hard to describe, how Wayne would empower people. He didn't codify it. He did it almost like breathing.

I'm very grateful to have worked for Wayne. He created an environment that enabled you to thrive and learn…He was an important role model—someone who could be so kind and caring and so successful. He inspired us. And he really did help us to stay so aligned together.[8]

Dan Paxton, who worked in a number of Human Resource executive roles during his career at PepsiCo, offered this insight:

Through his example, integrity, and genuine concern for people, Wayne engendered in the hearts of many of the leaders of PepsiCo a desire to be their very best, and to never let him down. I can honestly say I would walk over coals for that man, and there are very few leaders in the world today that I can say that about.[9]

Although we were a global company that was predominantly decentralized, in order for any individual to be able to move seamlessly from division to division, or country to country, or job to job, there needed to be a "cultural binding," so that regardless of division or country, the new assignment would always "feel" like PepsiCo. This is not unlike our Federalist model in the United States. Vermont is very different from California, which is vastly different than Texas. But a traveler recognizes familiarities and an overall shared culture, and feels comfortable moving from state to state.

It's worth emphasizing that, at PepsiCo, it was considered a badge of pride for any executive to give up the team's best talent, and to make sure that weak leaders would not get passed on to another unit. As we all appreciated, having the right talent—the best talent—was an essential element in PepsiCo's ability to fulfill its growth agenda and deliver with consistency.

CULTURE MATTERS

In order for PepsiCo to successfully utilize the "Federal" business model and the resulting matrix organizational structure, which inevitably also entailed lots of white space and ambiguity, there was a strong need for cultural cohesiveness. Roles and responsibilities and "Rules of the Road" can only go so far. In any organization, the real cohesion must be driven by culture and values. The dominant cultural bias at PepsiCo for decades was "results and integrity." That simple two-word description of the culture caused us to recruit, retain, and reward a targeted talent profile for the leadership team.

When explaining this simple formula for a successful culture, most people's reaction might be that "results" is not a value, and every culture expects people to be honest. However, when people would listen to Wayne talk about what these words really meant to the company and its success, it made perfect sense.

He described this within the big picture context for PepsiCo in his July 1994 speech at the Mars/Hostess/Frito-Lay Luncheon:

I'd like to…[tell] you about what I think is important in a business, any business, PepsiCo's big business, your business here in Canada, or some mom and pop food store way out there in Alberta. It's the five things I think we must get right everywhere if we want to succeed. These are things I believe we must do perfectly…

First: we must watch the consumer. It's important that we

do excellent market research [but] it's even more important that we watch how consumers react to things once they are in the marketplace. We need experienced managers who understand when real changes are taking place in the marketplace at any given moment in time. Our eyes must focus at point of sale.

The second: product. It may seem obvious, but big companies sometimes forget that products drive all consumer interest. If the products are appropriate, well-focused, good value, high quality, it's almost impossible to miss…

Third: talent—great people. You just can't do anything without terrific people in all key positions. If you don't have them, get them.

The fourth: personal accountability, or what I sometimes call "results orientation." Everybody must understand, at all times, we are accountable for very specific results and we'll be judged on how we achieve those results. Results count.

Fifth, and last on this short list, is integrity—corporate and personal.

Let me start with results as a value. The origins of this, and therefore the core approach, were set by the corporation's co-founders, Herman Lay and Don Kendall, who were both hardcore entrepreneurs. They came to play every day and played to win. They were risk-takers who were focused on creating the future, being willing to fail, and able to quickly recover. Being courageous and accountable, and most of all setting and achieving aggressive results, were what mattered most.

When Wayne took over Frito-Lay from Harold Lilley (who succeeded Herman Lay), and then at PepsiCo, when he replaced

Don Kendall, he stepped into a very large and already very successful global corporation. As a more general observation, it's the tendency of many first generation "professional executives," who step in and succeed a corporation's founders, to set up the structures and controls that a multi-billion dollar enterprise might seem to require.

That approach can cause a big shift from the wide-open "Playing to Win" model to a more controlled "Playing Not to Lose" approach: causing a rupture that can take a lean, explosive growth company and transform it into a conservative and slow, risk-averse enterprise.

Calloway and his executive team made the active choice to continue the entrepreneurial, results-oriented growth strategies. By doing so, they set PepsiCo on a clear course that attracted one type of talent and repelled another. If that's not a cultural paradigm, I don't know what is. In order to grow we had to attract people who "wanted the ball." We had to enable the notion of "batting averages" as opposed to perfection at every endeavor, and we were willing to take chances on putting people in charge of a business, a product, a plant or a department, often very early in their careers. For example, Roger Enrico, who eventually became Chairman of PepsiCo after Calloway, ran Pepsi-Cola Japan at age 29. This was in keeping with the cofounders' original approach. After all, Don Kendall was Chairman of PepsiCo when he was in his early 40s.

Bureaucracy was anathema to Wayne Calloway and the corporate culture that he helped institutionalize and grow. As far back as 1987, here's what he told an audience at Wichita State University, where he was serving as Executive in Residence: "We offer a company where bureaucracy is reduced to the lowest level we can stand. The only buck that's passed at PepsiCo is the paycheck."

Here's how he described the importance of the connection between the right environment and the right kind of people at PepsiCo, in a speech he delivered seven years later at Sacred Heart University:

> You can't expect people to do big things if they don't have big freedom and big opportunity. And that gets at my next point. It takes very special people to achieve the kind of growth we strive for at PepsiCo. Whether it's a division president or local route driver, we need people who are bright and ambitious, of course. But, equally important, people who are flexible, creative, open to change. People who are relentlessly focused on the needs of the customer, and willing to go out on a limb to meet those needs. We need people who are comfortable with a lot of autonomy, and confident enough to take action. Because unless we take action, we don't grow.

Steve Reinemund recalled:

> There was so much excitement. What drew me to PepsiCo was the idea that you could be a leader, develop a team, be supported by a large company but manage your operation as if it were a small company. You had autonomy. And once you signed on, Wayne was there to support and encourage you.[10]

And here's how Peggy Moore described this experience:

> I'm very grateful to have had the experience of being at PepsiCo during this era and working so closely with Wayne. He created a truly unique environment that enabled you to thrive and to learn. One wonderful part of it was, he showed you that it was possible to be such a good person and such a caring person

and also so successful.

Under Wayne, you took care of people, you didn't hurt people, and yet you also were part of this organization that had such a fabulous performance. He was such a powerful role model. He kept us so closely aligned. And he inspired us.[11]

The energy of youthful, smart, hardworking, ambitious people was palpable. Everywhere you went in PepsiCo, even in HR, Finance, and Information Technology, it was exciting to be part of it—so long as this was the right culture fit for you. It was painful if that wasn't the case. However, if you were not the right fit, you wouldn't last long. You would either be forced out or in many cases self-select to leave. And that was all part of the process and system that helped to ensure that people were aligned to the growth agenda and committed to results and integrity.

That said, despite the fact that PepsiCo's was an aggressively growth-oriented culture, it is important to emphasize that it was not a reckless, wide-open, Wild West town. That's where the second major value, "integrity," came into play, since it served as the stabilizing rudder.

In a 1994 interview, Calloway described what he meant by "integrity."

You've heard me say many times that the two foundations of good business are getting results and integrity, so we've got to have both of those rocks. You can probably get results in the short term, many times, without the integrity piece.

But if you're going to get results for the long term, which is where we are, we want to be here 100 years from now. We talk about the "50-year solution" sometimes as we make decisions about businesses and about people. To do that long term, you're clearly going to have to have the integrity piece.

By that, I mean the broadest sense of the word. Obviously, we don't want people stealing and working the books, but integrity means openness, honesty, caring about other people, being willing to share in the rewards as well as the challenges and being willing to sacrifice perhaps some of your own personal goals for the team goals and those are the kinds of things that we mean about integrity.

Throughout my career, I've heard many leaders say the words "caring, openness, and honesty," when, in fact, these concepts were not consistently applied. For Wayne, it was not rhetoric, particularly when you were in a business like ours, where we had millions and millions of transactions every day and were operating in more than 150 countries[12] with different kinds of businesses. The string that bound everything together was the integrity and the trust and the buying into the company's values. No one could supervise 400,000 people every day. You can't go back and check. You can't follow it up. Those are the kind of situations in which people just have to be responsible. You have to trust the people in order for you to give them the responsibility to do what they have to do.

Years after Wayne Calloway passed away, it's remarkable how many people still talk about his commitment to integrity as a foundational leadership—and personal—principle. So it's not surprising that there are many eloquent examples of his discussions of this, not only to the PepsiCo community, but when he delivered speeches to audiences of outside business groups, stock market analysts, students, or others.

In an April 1994 speech at the PepsiCo Personnel Conference, he commented:

> I suggest we all work harder on what some people call the "soft" side of the equation. I call it integrity. By that I mean honesty, openness, trust, equality, mutual respect, self-respect, dignity, teamwork, recognition. Or, you might call it caring...
>
> [T]hese are the basic values that we live by every day. These are the values that let us make the necessary quick decisions in a decentralized organization. These are the values that allow us to take risks and try new things—embrace continuous transformation.
>
> Think about it. People who are honest don't play corporate politics. People who trust the people who work for them make good leaders because they are willing to empower the people who work for them. People who trust the people around them are willing to take risks and try new things, and not worry about getting sandbagged. People who have mutual respect for others work for the team. They share in the rewards when we win, and in the responsibility when we lose.

Olden Lee, who worked closely with him in roles that included serving as Senior Vice President of Human Resources for Taco Bell and Senior Vice President & Chief Personnel Officer at the KFC division, shared a revealing anecdote:

> We were doing a work group survey. I was reporting back the results of the senior managers survey [to Wayne] and I came to one question: "We think the company operates with integrity." We were at 98.2% [of people who agreed with this statement]. Wayne said, "That's a good score. But almost 2% of our senior managers don't think we operate with integrity—and

when our senior people don't feel that way, we have a problem."

I thought about that. His response showed me how much Wayne, and consequently all of us, should value integrity. Three or four weeks later, I asked him, "What are your thoughts regarding integrity: is it an honesty question?"

He said, "No. We don't tolerate dishonest people. They'd be gone. My primary concern with integrity is people doing what they say they're going to do. If you commit to something in the company, you'd better get it done, because a lot of people are depending on you—and if you can't do it, you'd better speak up."

In retrospect, I have thought that this was a simple but profound way of looking at it [that is, integrity]: do what you say you will do.[13]

To let Wayne have the last say on this truly essential aspect of organizational (and personal) excellence, here are his comments from a speech that he delivered at a Mars/Hostess/Frito-Lay luncheon in July 1994:

[Integrity is] something I've talked about at every meeting I've attended in the last decade and I can't say it often enough. Integrity—on both the personal and corporate level—means honesty, of course, but a lot more: fairness, openness, candor, consistency. It means the absence of hidden agendas.

Integrity is the one thing that allows you to operate without "big company-itis." It allows you to loosen the reins, drop the memos-for-the-record. It lets everybody swing from the heels. Integrity stimulates trust—and trust fuels the corporate engine.

There was an additional dimension to the culture that supported "Results and Integrity." For lack of a better term, I'll call it the "magic." Think about those intangibles that make the Yankees' pinstripes or Notre Dame's golden helmet special. For those of us who worked at PepsiCo during this era, there was the feeling of belonging to something that was deeply special, and caring about the team and each other in a way that made us want to get up in the morning, go to work, and do our very best to exceed expectations.

It started with that feeling that you are part of something special. You felt that, as tough as the neighborhood is, these people are your neighbors and friends. That feeling emanated from Wayne and, his cherished wife, Jan Calloway, and it radiated to every level in the company, from the gracious dinner parties, to the annual retreats that included spouses, to encouraging participation in our communities and charities.

As Indra Nooyi, PepsiCo's Chairman and CEO, recalled:

Wayne cared deeply for PepsiCo and its people. He really was PepsiCo and everything he did was aimed at building up the people and the organization. He wanted everyone to succeed together.

Wayne and Jan together were a great reflection of the care and love that we all felt for the organization. Jan was so much a part of what made PepsiCo great during this period. They were a powerful team and they were truly outstanding representatives of PepsiCo.[14]

This was clear to so many of us who had the privilege and the pleasure of interacting with Wayne and Jan during this exciting period. One of the remarkable things about them was they made everyone feel special. My wife, Cindy, and I went to New York every October to celebrate our wedding anniversary. Every year they would insist that we stay at their home in Greenwich, CT for the weekend. They rolled out the red carpet with everything from flowers in our room, to dinner parties with our PepsiCo friends, to just laying around and reading the newspapers together on Sunday morning. To this day I don't know whether we were extra special or if they made everyone feel that way. I suspect the latter was the case. That takes not just energy, but a true loving spirit that was part of their magic. Here's how Steve Reinemund described it:

> It wasn't just Wayne. Jan was a big part of the culture too. In all due respect—because I loved the man dearly—it's fair to say that he was not the most social of animals. But Jan would put the pizzazz into whatever we did within a work-related social environment—leadership retreats, dinner parties, and more. She knew how to support Wayne's business responsibilities and activities and priorities in ways that were incredibly effective.[15]

There was a pride and a feeling of inclusion that was distinctively PepsiCo. You and your family felt at home and immediately adjusted to a new job or division or location anywhere on the globe. Chances were pretty good that you would have already worked with, or at least knew, someone who would be part of your work life in your new job.

In addition to these softer notions, there were a number of Human Resources innovations that Calloway pushed. For example, since he wanted all the 400,000 or so employees to act like owners, he introduced "SharePower," a benefit that made everyone a shareholder with options, because you only made money if the price went up.

Wayne also believed that if you worked hard, you should play hard—and that required you to be in shape—so he invested in some of the earliest corporate fitness centers. The quality of those facilities was only surpassed by the quality of the programs and staff.

Wayne felt that PepsiCo's leaders and their teams should be aware of the big issues of our times, so we had world-class speakers, who included members of Congress, Senators, economists and historians. It was an intellectually interesting, challenging, and rewarding environment: one that had a palpably strong culture that was meticulously tended to by Calloway, Kendall (the founding Chairman and CEO), Roger Enrico (the Chairman and CEO who succeeded Wayne), Mike Jordan (CEO, PepsiCo Foods), and John Ewing, Roger King, William Bensyl, and David Zemelman (all HR leaders).

At an "Experiencing PepsiCo" speech in September 1994, Wayne offered a vision of our community that would have made any of us proud:

> Our most successful ventures are driven by straight shooters, people you can trust, people you enjoy working with because you're not afraid to turn your back. People who live for innovation and continuous improvement. Together, these special qualities allow us to grow and stretch and achieve whatever we're capable of.

This was PepsiCo's internal "brand," and in many cases it reflected the fun, exciting, external brand image. Truly, we were the "Pepsi Generation."

LEADERSHIP MATTERS

By now there should be no confusion as to why leadership matters. As discussed earlier, every leader sets an agenda. But sometimes this is accomplished more effectively than other times. And sometimes, even the most promising of agendas don't last very long. Picture the number of enterprises that set a new and fundamentally different agenda every time they change the leader, or anytime events don't go as planned. Conversely, there's a different kind of problem that also surfaces all too frequently, when incumbent leaders continue with their same agenda, no matter how significantly conditions change.

The fact is, thousands, hundreds of thousands, and in the case of a nation, millions of people rise or fall based on those agendas. It's worth pointing out that leaders also set the structure, performance standards, and culture for any organization. Get those right and you have an energetic workforce that is filled with trust, opportunity, hope, and joy. If you get all this right, you'll achieve consistent results. So, it all does come down to the quality of leadership.

Some might say that too much rests on a leader's shoulders. After all, no single individual is perfect at every aspect of leadership. No leader can be great at marketing, manufacturing, sales, and all the other key functions that contribute to organizational success. No single leader can be the absolute best at picking talent or be an inspiring communicator. And, most importantly, no leader can be everywhere, all of the time, or make every decision (unless we're looking at a tiny mom and pop operation or a fledging entrepreneurial venture). Meanwhile, founders retire, enterprises reach scale, and globalization alone demands that leaders delegate responsibilities in a process that gets replicated again and again throughout an organization.

In organizations in which too much power is concentrated in the hands of a single leader (or small number of leaders), leadership transitions can be especially difficult and disruptive. But at PepsiCo there was a belief that leadership teams—not just talented individuals—were the winning formula. A team of leaders that ran a division, country operation, or a department was carefully constructed to enhance strengths and offset the weakness of each talented individual, not unlike what happens with a sports team. At PepsiCo, a winning team was as much about spirit, culture, and competitiveness (and, oh yes, by the way, you do need talented players).

Given the PepsiCo DNA, when it came time for Don Kendall to step down, he had a huge base of talented leaders to choose from. It's worth emphasizing that Kendall and Calloway had very different personas. Don was exuberant and a force of nature. Wayne was reserved and humble. But they both had the same passion for "Results and Integrity." They both believed in an aggressive growth agenda and they shared a strong competitive fire. They also both believed that winning was a team sport and that leaders who you recruited, developed, rotated, promoted, and managed out would be the key to long-term success.

When Calloway left Frito-Lay in 1983 and went to PepsiCo, he actually advanced and accelerated the concept that success depended on hiring and developing lots and lots of strong, creative leaders. He accomplished this, not by issuing an edict or sending out a memo. Instead, he personally set the pace and the standards for who was hired and promoted. He personally was involved and met with anyone who was a serious contender for any of the top few hundred jobs. He participated as actively in Human Resource

Planning (HRP) as he did in the Capital Expenditures (CAPEX) processes.

In other words, he put his calendar time where he felt it really mattered, which included both how the company allocated financial funds and who got to lead which part of the corporation. And that delivered a huge and lasting impact. Joe McCann articulated what many of us still feel today:

> I'm not exaggerating when I say that Wayne was the greatest boss you could imagine. He never got ruffled. He never blamed you for mistakes. If you were incompetent, it's true, he somehow would find the right way to get rid of you, but he even did that in a nice way. He was so gentlemanly, so quiet, so supportive.[16]

Peggy Moore also recalled this trait of his:

> It didn't matter where you were in the organization—he would listen to you. He would take what you had to say seriously. Often he would try to find ways to act on your advice. He was committed to the notion of mutual trust. And as a result of all that, people throughout the organization trusted him.[17]

Beyond the top 500 leaders that Wayne personally knew and spent time with, he required those 500 leaders to do the same thing with more than 10,000 managers across every division. Even more important than the quarterly assessment that I discussed earlier, each PepsiCo leader had an individual, multi-year development plan. That plan might call for some formal training, but it also would involve adding new responsibilities or a key assignment in another function, division or geography to broaden that person. It

was the normal course of business to move a Pepsi-Cola marketing executive to a manufacturing job, or a Kentucky Fried Chick-
en field manager to headquarters, or a corporate finance person to
an international post.

This was a massive system of building next generation leaders
who could manage a function or a P&L. Roughly one-quarter of
the leadership population was promoted to new and growing responsibilities each and every year.

Steve Reinemund shared a personal anecdote that does a great
job of illustrating just how involved and engaged Wayne Calloway
was in all of the various pieces that came together to help build
this leadership corps:

> At one time, I was running a club for million-dollar managers.
> The first time we had a big event, I asked Wayne and Jan to
> travel to join us there—and I asked Wayne to present the rings
> and jackets to these managers. I'll admit this: that first time we
> did it, the event was really not as well planned as it could have
> been and it seemed to take forever.
>
> So I apologized to Wayne. After all, he was the CEO of the
> whole company. But he told me that there was no reason to
> apologize. He said that it was the most important thing that
> we could do to recognize those managers and their accom-
> plishments.[18]

PepsiCo was an exciting place to learn and grow, but that
sometimes meant moving people out of the company who were
blocking key positions. Sometimes it meant picking up your family and moving to another part of the globe if you had the ambition
and adventurous spirit. However, it was not career-limiting if you
chose to pass up an opportunity, as I did.

It's hard to imagine how someone who manages a $20+ billion global enterprise could have had the time to interview and assess candidates, and otherwise be involved in so much HR work. But, that's exactly the point. If you buy into the notion that people play such an enormous role in your success, this *is* how you manage the business.

Given the importance that he placed in every aspect of the HR process, it's not surprising that Wayne tried to inspire this team with a vision of how recruitment and talent management strategies would need to evolve, along with PepsiCo's growth and changing conditions throughout the global marketplace. In a speech at the PepsiCo Personnel Conference in April 1994, he emphasized:

> So, here's the challenge [to HR]. Right now, in the spirit of continual transformation, I'd like to ask three things of you: Be more aggressive. Be more flexible. Be more insightful.
>
> We have to be a *lot* more aggressive in recruiting, hiring, and developing people. The needs are too great, the numbers too big, the market too competitive, for us to do it any other way. And we don't just need more great people. We need a much wider range of great people. As our business becomes more international, our workforce will look less like the United States and more like the United Nations...
>
> Just how diverse can an organization be—and still work effectively toward a common goal? For that matter, in a more diverse world, should we search for people who think exactly like us, but may look or sound different? Or should we look for people who are different in much more fundamental ways?
>
> I'd say we're probably looking for both. That's why it's so vitally important to be flexible. I'm certain we can have

an organization that is both broadly diverse and highly competitive in the marketplace. But we have to be flexible enough to accommodate a dramatically wide range of people in our organization...

Now, being more aggressive and flexible will help us to accelerate the process of finding and developing the best people. But the third part of my challenge, being more insightful, is what will truly enable us to recognize...the hundreds of other gifted leaders we will need. As the people side of our businesses grows more complex, as we draw from a far broader universe of people, greater insight into human potential will give us tremendous advantage. We must become better judges of people. Our challenge will be to look beyond the suit, beyond the voice, beyond the outward characteristics to find the people who can really contribute to, and grow with, PepsiCo.

This focus on talented, results-oriented, aggressive leaders was only part of the PepsiCo magic. Other terrific companies also attracted great talent from the best schools during the '70s, '80s, and '90s. But they created very different work environments than we had. Our structure, consisting of independent divisions and operating units, produced the Federal model described earlier, which put the power to decide, innovate, succeed, fail, and recover into the field operating units. At PepsiCo, we had literally hundreds of General Managers by the 1990s and 35 individual businesses that were large enough to be in the Fortune 500 all by themselves. This is where the Talent and Performance Management Systems produced such powerful results, creating an environment that served as a real breeding ground in which people were able to progress by accepting more and more responsibility quite early in their careers.

Wayne gave people as much as they could handle—rising leaders such as Steve Reinemund, who was the CEO of Pizza Hut at 38, or Chris Sinclair, who ran Pepsi-Cola International at 38. That talent machine was in our corporate DNA. Don Kendall, who had become CEO of PepsiCo at 44, believed that putting bright, talented people into stretch roles would make our business exciting—and exciting businesses are growth businesses. So the people strategy aligned with, reinforced, and enabled the business strategy.

When you run this kind of wide-open offense and give people freedom to try new things, you also have to give them the freedom to fail. At a 1987 Executive in Residence speech at Wichita State University, Wayne emphasized:

> We don't want our employees to be afraid to take a risk. We want employees to know that the company will support them. It's OK to make mistakes so long as they learn something from them. We punish incompetence—we don't punish mistakes if people can learn from them. If we did we'd grind to a halt.

So does that mean that if you give people the wherewithal to do great things, you're destined never to get a good night's sleep?

Put another way, when you put together lots of bright, creative, motivated people, give them lots of responsibility, set very ambitious goals, and then give them tremendous freedom, how do you prevent anarchy? What keeps the place from falling apart?

In Wayne's opinion, the answer boiled down to Results and Integrity.

NOTES

1. PepsiCo, Inc, "1996 Selected Financial Data," http://www.pepsico.com/Annual-Reports/1996/selecteddata.html.

2. Charlie Feld, *Blind Spot: A Leader's Guide to IT-Enabled Business Transformation* (Dallas: Olive Press, 2009).

3. Constance L. Hays, "Wayne Calloway Dies at 62; Was Chief at PepsiCo 10 Years," *The New York Times*, July 10, 1998.

4. Jack Welch, Interview, 2014.

5. Joe McCann, Interview, 2014.

6. Indra K. Nooyi, Interview, 2014.

7. "Former PepsiCo CEO Wayne Calloway Dies. Industry Executives Praise His Leadership." *Beverage Digest*, July 7, 1998. http://www.beverage-digest.com/editorial/980717.html.

8. Peggy Moore, Interview, 2014.

9. Dan Paxton, Interview, 2014.

10. Steve Reinemund, Interview, 2014.

11. Peggy Moore, Interview, 2014.

12. PepsiCo, Inc., "Our History." http://www.pepsico.com/Company/Our-History.

13. Olden Lee, Interview, 2014.

14. Indra K. Nooyi, Interview, 2014.

15. Steve Reinemund, Interview, 2014.

16. Joe McCann, Interview, 2014.

17. Peggy Moore, Interview, 2014.

18. Steve Reinemund, Interview, 2014.

CONCLUSION

THE BOTTOM LINE IN LEADERSHIP

WHEN WAYNE CALLOWAY SPOKE ABOUT RESULTS, he meant that everyone in the organization was judged on one thing: the results he or she achieved. No politics. No excuses. Just results. Real, specific, measurable results. At PepsiCo, we judged people on what they achieved, not what college they had gone to or what kind of haircut they had. The people who moved ahead were those who achieved superior results. But, it's important to stress, this was not the kind of culture that wanted results at any cost.

Sure, we wanted results, but we wanted them the right way. Sure, we were committed to growth, but not at the expense of our character.

That's where integrity comes in. It was the glue that held everything together. And, as I have stressed throughout this book, he made it clear to everyone within the organization that this was the bedrock of both his leadership principles and PepsiCo's extraordinary culture.

For those of us who worked with him, during that special era, within that special corporation, we embraced a deep and lifelong appreciation of the fact that integrity didn't just refer to the obvious things, like stealing or cooking the books. What Wayne and PepsiCo meant by integrity was an openness, an honesty, a frank way of doing business. He would often talk about core objectives that were essential elements of integrity, such as consistency, trust, and the fundamental need to respect people.

John Ewing, who served as a Senior Vice President at Frito-Lay, shared this insight in his interview: "He never forgot where his roots were and where he came from and his warmth and his humility, in my opinion, were his great assets."[1]

As I've said, he wasn't much of a talker. But he was an exceptionally effective communicator—not only because he listened so attentively to people and thought so carefully about what they were saying—but because he was consistent and clear in terms of his own messages about what really mattered. When a leader returns to certain messages again and again, both inside an organization and outside, there can be no doubt about what matters most. With Calloway, integrity and results were themes that wove their way through his speeches and conversations year after year. If you were part of the team at PepsiCo, you understood why they were important and you shared his commitment.

It was an environment that was deeply rewarding, but also challenging and complex. During my years at PepsiCo, the very nature of our organizational style produced a vast amount of white space. Differences of opinion were the norm and each leader was passionate about beliefs and positions. Debates were encouraged until the point at which decisions were made. Of course, even as a leader, you never knew which way things would go. Sometimes your views would prevail, sometimes they wouldn't. But what was not debatable was your integrity. There were no shades of gray.

Your sense of integrity was like a light switch, it was either on or off; you had it or you didn't. Everyone knew that though people within the organization can agree or disagree, there has got to be trust. In other words, you might disagree with my beliefs, but we're both genuine in our beliefs and desired approach and, therefore, we can trust and respect each other and know that there are no hidden agendas. He constantly referred to this value as "intellectual integrity."

This approach was exhibited very publically at PepsiCo so as to reinforce it as a leadership value. In the early 1980s, a team of international executives "cooked the books" as they say, in order to cover up a blunder. Don Kendall, Andy Pearson, and Wayne Calloway immediately made the issue very public, took the write-off and summarily replaced the management team. This damaged the stock price, but it also reinforced the difference between honest, aggressive mistakes and crossing the line. They could have taken a different PR-focused route and handled the problem in ways that would have been more subtle and gradual, but that would not have been the "PepsiCo Way." They made it very clear and widely known within the organization that a financial plan miss, while not acceptable, would have been survivable. This behavior was not.

For me, and for so many of the men and women with whom I worked at PepsiCo during the Calloway era, we were influenced and inspired in ways that have shaped our whole lives. This book has attempted to cover a great deal of ground, because we feel that there are so many important lessons that can be learned from Wayne's leadership and PepsiCo's many achievements during this period. But there were also, as I have tried to suggest, so many intangibles. There truly was something magic about Wayne and the great corporation that he led. No book can ever fully convey just how deeply fortunate we were to have been involved in all this in a first-hand way.

For those who are reading this book in search of its timeless leadership lessons: without results and integrity, no organization can survive over a long period of time. This was true then and is still true today. The pace of change and the speed of business has certainly accelerated, but these values and this leadership model are still the bedrock in building a great organization. PepsiCo survived and thrived despite the competitive "wars," the economic cycles and consistently changing consumer preference through the '70s, '80s and '90s because, in the end, leadership talent and a culture of results and integrity trump all else. In Calloway's PepsiCo, it was well known, understood, and basically considered to be a leadership given that all action was based upon the cornerstones of results and integrity

As I conclude these pages, I find myself recalling so many of Wayne's messages to his leadership team. Set high standards and stick to them. Give people the freedom to do what they are capable of. Measure them fairly, based on results. Create an atmosphere of integrity, and provide people with the opportunity to achieve and succeed.

No wonder PepsiCo was such a great breeding ground for the best of the human spirit.

* * *

As I mentioned in the earliest pages of this book, I did not embark upon this project lightly. Having already written one book, it was not my intention to write another.

But I was driven by two motivations. The first was a strong desire to turn the spotlight on a great and impactful chief executive, Wayne Calloway, and an exciting and rewarding era in the history of the great corporation he led, PepsiCo. Both are deserving of enormous respect and credit, and it is my hope that I have conveyed this to my readers.

I had a second, powerful motivation as well, which was to examine a proven model of leadership that I believe could hold great value for business and society alike, during an era in which we have been handicapped by the shortcomings of too many of our current crop of leaders. Many of them lack courage or vision, or both of these essential qualities. Rather than inspiring us to work together toward common, significant goals, they confuse, divide, and weaken us.

Today's businesses and other organizations face many risks and challenges, as well as opportunities. For societies and individuals as well, this is also the case. Transformation may be inevitable for us all, but it is hard. It's frightening. It's confusing.

Yet, at a time when leadership has never been more important for all of us, we face a profound leadership crisis. As I have tried to argue throughout these pages, we are in desperate need of a leadership renaissance. We need to learn from those individuals and leadership models that have proven their value over time.

All of which brings me back to Wayne Calloway and his more than 25 years of leadership at PepsiCo. I believe that they hold meaningful lessons for all of us, whether in terms of the leaders we choose or the strategies that our leaders rely upon.

As I have described throughout these pages, for many of my former colleagues, as well as myself: we have moved on to careers outside PepsiCo, but we have remained part of a great fraternity and heritage. Most of us have been extremely successful in life and in our careers, in large part because of what we learned about leadership, setting and achieving important goals, and building great teams from our years with Wayne Calloway and PepsiCo.

We learned how to appreciate, nurture, and sustain integrity within a results-oriented culture built upon teamwork and accomplishment.

Wayne Calloway and PepsiCo inspired and aligned us to work together to achieve those objectives that mattered most. They don't offer all the answers, of course. But I firmly believe that we all have much to learn from them today.

As I conclude these pages, with the strongest of hopes that my readers have come to share this perspective, I salute Wayne Calloway and the great global corporation he led.

NOTES

1. John Ewing, Interview, 2014.